SEEKING
BALANCE

SEEKING BALANCE

JOHN MCGORY

Book Design & Production
Columbus Publishing Lab
www.ColumbusPublishingLab.com

Paperback ISBN: 978-1-63337-308-2
E-book ISBN: 978-1-63337-309-9

Printed in the United States of America

1   2   3   4   5   6   7   8   9   0

Dedicated to my large family and many friends from around the world who share with me the beauty and joy of spoken English…

I love you all.

I also want to thank The Ohio State University, Ohio University and Jianghan University for helping me as a student and teacher pursue my unique vision of excellence.

CONTENTS

INTRODUCTION
HOW TO USE THIS BOOK

Welcome, English speaker

WELCOME TO *SEEKING BALANCE*: The ultimate guide to English-speaking excellence for the shy, foreign or frustrated. Speaking English is so much more than simply getting the words in the right order. Achieving excellence is challenging. Speaking well requires solid strategy, controlled emotions, sharp social and physical skills, and a philosophical core.

I've spent my life talking as a professional spokesperson in government and business and an award-winning oral English teacher. This book shares strategies and tips I've learned and taught around the world.

TOP TIP
PURSUE EXCELLENCE, NOT SUCCESS.

This book lays out the basic beliefs, concepts, and attitudes of what I believe to be the core elements of communicating well in English. The underpinnings of my philosophy involve the ideas of acceptance, balance, and change in speaking English. I call this the ABC philosophy.

Let's break it down for you.

A. **ACCEPTANCE:** Effective communicators accept who they are as an individual and the world where they exist.

B. **BALANCE:** Effective communicators balance thoughts, ideas, and emotions in any situation. Imbalance creates discord which hinders communication.

C. **CHANGE:** Effective communicators seek change through building excellence not success. The third element involves an individual's ability to accept and incorporate positive change into communicating. These sought-after improvements include balance, strategies, body language, and mindfulness.

Introduction

Our ABC philosophy provides an easy-to-follow approach to accepting, balancing, and changing an individual's English-speaking ability.

People who chase success will discover that it is fleeting as a beautiful sunset. Today you're ablaze in glory, tomorrow forgotten. Success involves comparing your life to others and those comparisons shift like the desert sands.

The pursuit of excellence, however, remains wherever you go. Maximizing your gifts, talents, and abilities to perform at the highest potential builds confidence and sustainability in whatever endeavor you pursue.

The book's lessons focus on becoming your best. Don't compare your skills and talents to others but work towards being the finest speaker you can be. Realize that your competitor is the person who looks back at you in the mirror. Get better than the person looking at you today and life opens up like a flower.

Don't waste time worrying about others but strive to improve and success will find you.

Seeking Balance looks at the act of speaking English like an athlete studies how to improve personal skills. A world-class athlete strives to improve in these four key areas:

1. The body
2. Mental strength
3. Game situations and strategies
4. Practice drills

The athlete seeks to perfect individual skills in practice. Then in competition they do their best and let the results tell the story. Winning isn't as important as peak performance. They congratulate their opponent win or lose and then go back to work. This book provides readers with the same framework for excelling in speaking English.

Seeking Balance uses the writings and thoughts of Lao Tzu from his transformational book *Tao Te Ching* (*The Book of the Way and Virtue*). The masterpiece has influenced Taoism, Buddhism and other philosophical beliefs throughout the world for centuries.

A kung fu fighter or a tai chi master uses centuries-old Tao philosophy to build mental strength and physical control. This book uses the same approach.

TOP TIP
SPEAK ENGLISH LIKE A KUNG FU FIGHTER USING MENTAL STRENGTH AND PHYSICAL CONTROL AS CORE STRENGTHS.

Feel free to use the guide as a reference book to improve specific areas of speech. If you want to skip around and focus on certain segments, then that's OK!

Talking involves interaction between at least two people. This book provides numerous suggested activities, practice exercises, discussion questions, and model conversations that encourage a team approach.

Potential working partnerships include friends, coworkers, parents, grandparents, and classmates. Most lessons from the book can be easily understood by individuals over the age of twelve years old.

Shared experiences ensure improvement and strengthen personal relationships. So put in the work with others to improve while building positive bonds.

The book's eight sections allow readers to concentrate on the parts of spoken English that need the most attention. The sections are:

1. SEEKING BALANCE: A discussion of the importance of balance in speaking, with an emphasis on ideas from ancient Chinese culture.
2. CHANGE: A powerful section on how to incorporate change into your life.

3. THE BODY AND TALKING: A focus on movement and how we use the body in talking.

4. SITUATIONS: Talking involves common situations. This book studies ten everyday conversations and provides useful suggestions.

5. TALKING STRATEGIES: Sound strategy when talking increases chances for excellence. This section provides a look at modern science and makes recommendations for a sound talking strategy.

6. PERSONAL GROWTH: This section contains easy-to-follow activities that improve the reader's speaking ability. These improvements can facilitate employability, enhance the quality of life, and contribute to the realization of dreams and aspirations.

7. TIPS: Three hundred sixty-six talking tips that give a year's worth of ideas on improving talking skills.

8. APPENDIX: The appendix contains two blank documents, the Talking Improvement Plan and the Personal Talking Brand. These allow readers to develop personal improvement strategies.

Use this guide as a structured improvement program or an occasional reference guide to improve English-speaking capabilities in specific situations.

My hope is that the book brings you joy in your pursuit of spoken English excellence.

John McGory
Wuhan, China
June 2019

SEEKING BALANCE

SHARING IDEAS AND THOUGHTS

THIS BOOK SERVES AS A GUIDE for shy, foreign or frustrated English speakers who wish to achieve excellence in interpersonal communication.

This book approaches speaking English like an athletic contest. The best contestants use excellent technique in body awareness, mental strength, strategies, and practice. This requires discarding old ways of doing things.

TOP TIP
LEARN TO UNLEARN UNPRODUCTIVE HABITS.

As babies we're taught how to think, act, and talk. Some lessons were good, others not so much. Well, let's start fresh. Our hope is that you can slowly eliminate unproductive childhood lessons and incorporate new ideas about speaking English.

Balance

The key physical quality of any world-class athlete regardless of the sport is balance. This ability allows an athlete to always respond in an appropriate fashion. A football player, a gymnast, a ping-pong player, and a kung fu fighter are just a few examples of athletes who use balance to compete.

Speaking English requires the same skill. A speaker needs to be prepared in all situations to respond in an appropriate manner. Poor balance while talking causes any number of problems from anger to insecurity. So what do we mean by speaking "balance"? The definition of balance we use is:

Balance: A condition in which different elements are equal or in the correct proportions.

In athletics, this requires an equal distribution of weight so the body can respond in any direction. In speaking, balance requires physical, mental, and emotional control which allows the speaker to properly respond.

The concept of balance influences conversations in two ways:

1. **INDIVIDUAL SPEAKING BALANCE:** The physical, mental, and emotional ability of a person to carry out their part of a conversation in an open, honest and entertaining way and

2. **CONVERSATION BALANCE:** Two (or more) people speaking in a conversation in correct proportions.

Conversations are two-way streets where different elements (people) attempt to be in correct proportions. A good conversation requires both parties to participate in more or less equal ways.

This book concentrates on individual speaking balance. Our collective goal is to improve staying steady and preparing for your half of the conversation bargain.

TOP TIP
YOU HAVE NO CONTROL OVER WHAT OTHERS SAY IN A CONVERSATION. FOCUS ON WHAT YOU CONTROL.

All we can ever achieve is *personal* balance. One of the fastest ways to lose balance in a conversation is to "expect" a person to say or act in a particular way. When that fails to happen we become surprised, angry, upset, or disturbed to some degree. We lose balance and many times the conversation quickly goes downhill.

We all want conversations where two people express thoughts, words, and emotions that reflect well-considered, honest and supportive viewpoints.

How often do we have such conversations? Who knows since you can never really tell if the other person's giving an honest viewpoint. People know how to talk without revealing much, leaving many conversations devoid of anything but misleading, deceptive, or boring self-centered comments.

A truly enlightened English speaker doesn't fall into this trap. They captivate all who talk with them. Their honesty refreshes, their viewpoints educate and entertain, and they express genuine interest in their talking partner.

So learn to unlearn by accepting the concept that the only person you control is you. Forget about trying to control the 7.5 billion people on earth and focus on you and your truly amazing skills.

Communication breakdown

The definition of communication is the conveying or sharing of ideas and feelings.

Shy, foreign, or frustrated speakers struggle with sharing information due to a number of factors. Let's look at a few examples of failing in the give-and-take of conversation.

The shy speaker, feeling embarrassed or inhibited to share thoughts with others, keeps quiet, not allowing for true interaction and balance. This leaves both parties unsatisfied with the interchange.

The English-as-a-second-language speaker believes they are at a disadvantage when talking with native English speakers. They listen carefully but often remain silent, holding back due to a lack of confidence in their English-speaking abilities.

The frustrated speaker gets caught up in situations that prevent the exchange of thoughts. Work, relationships, and life can create scenarios where honest conversation seems impossible. These situations leave the frustrated with a sense of disappointment, resentment, or anger.

TOP TIP
LEARN FROM EVERY CONVERSATION.

The problem with each of these scenarios is the shy, foreign, or frustrated speaker believes that they've "lost" the conversation. They see each interaction as a little game with an undeclared but clear winner and loser.

Speaking involves the flow of information back and forth between people. It is never a zero-sum game (A zero-sum game: Whatever one person gains from a situation the other person loses exactly that amount). Each person gains valuable information in a conversation.

A person who wrongly believes they are "losing" every conversation cannot help but feel that they lack the talent, emotional strength, or position in life to use the spoken word as a valuable tool.

Seeking Balance builds confidence step-by-step in shy, foreign, and frustrated speakers. ***You will become an excellent English speaker.*** But, yes, hurdles must be overcome.

The power in getting it right

Two of the world's most impactful people over the past 50 years are Warren Buffett and Queen Elizabeth II. They've shaped financial, political, and social life around the world.

Buffett and the Queen share a common belief that getting communication right plays a key role in success.

11

The Oracle of Omaha is one of America's most successful business-people. Buffett's unassuming approach belies his shrewd money-making ability which has earned him billions of dollars.

Buffett tells young college graduates that the most important skill successful people have is the ability to communicate. Buffett tells young students:

> **"At your young age the best way you can improve is to learn to communicate better... Without good communication skills you won't be able to convince people to follow you even though you see over the mountain and they don't."**

Carnegie Institute of Technology research found that a surprising 15 percent of financial success comes from knowledge and technical skills while 85 percent comes from the ability to effectively communicate, negotiate, and lead, using both speaking and listening skills.

The United Kingdom's Queen Elizabeth II said this about success:

> **"I know of no single formula for success. But over the years I have observed that some attributes of leadership are universal and are often about finding ways of encouraging people to combine their efforts, their talents, their insights, their enthusiasm, and their inspiration to work together."**

Many influential leaders agree that no matter what goals you have in life, whether business or personal, how well you communicate plays an important part in determining excellence.

Hurdles

Wanting to communicate and actually communicating are two very different things. Things get in the way like bad attitudes, sensitive feelings, or the unwillingness to share. Overcoming these hurdles determines conversation outcomes.

Polite communication encourages the use of a balanced, sharing approach, incorporating both respect and strength when communicating ideas and feelings.

Mastering both strong and respectful elements, however, is not an easy achievement. Most people are one but not the other. Strong speakers have no problem telling others their thoughts while seeming incapable of showing legitimate respect by listening.

Very respectful speakers come off as timid, struggling to say anything. The inability to share thoughts and words gets them trampled or forgotten. When they attempt to speak with strength, people laugh or ignore them. So, they weakly say "excuse me" and "I'm sorry" while getting pushed aside or overlooked by the world.

The struggle continues.

English speaking, Chinese philosophy

I started teaching oral English at Jianghan University in Wuhan, China in 2014 after years as an American business and political communicator. It didn't take long to realize the stark difference between Chinese and Western hemisphere speakers.

The Chinese, quiet but kind once a relationship develops, tread lightly with others, understanding the importance of not losing face in conversation. The biggest conversation mistake in China involves making disparaging public comments to another. They keep intentions hidden, often talking around a subject rather than getting to the point.

Western speakers, on the other hand, are likely to be more open, revealing intentions within a short period of time. Unlike the Chinese, they may "get in your face" and "tell it like it is."

Westerners living in China struggle when confronting the Chinese over issues. I've seen teachers blame university officials for problems, only to be shunned or fired for their harsh words. This very un-Chinese style simply isn't accepted. The dismissed teacher never figures out what went wrong.

Both styles of conversation hold value. But, when in another country, a speaker must remember they are a visitor. The adage, "when in Rome, do as the Romans do," should be amended to say "when in Rome, speak as the Romans speak."

So how does a speaker deal with conflicting concepts of communication? Can an American's zero-sum game style and the Chinese circumspect style live in peace?

My belief is yes, they can coexist. In fact, I believe the two concepts can thrive as one so I wrote *Seeking Balance*. This book provides a roadmap for the shy, foreign and frustrated to balance strength and respect into one powerful English-speaking concept.

All emotions lie within

A good communicator acknowledges all emotions exist within. How many times do you say?

- "I'm shy"
- "He's mean"
- "What an angry person"
- "I'm funny"

While the statements may reflect an individual's demeanor at that moment, they hide the existence of opposite qualities. Every person is shy and outgoing, mean and nice, angry and happy, or funny and serious.

TOP TIP
ALL EMOTIONS ARE WITHIN YOU:
HAPPY AND SAD; SHY AND OPEN; FUN AND SERIOUS.

Chinese philosophy believes in the singular nature of the universe. All of us are simply a part of one. All qualities, all emotions, all beliefs reside in you. We are a part of the universe and we are the universe.

Do you see yourself as a one-side-of-the-coin speaker? Do you believe you're only shy or only pushy? Kind or strong? Angry or anxious?

Excellent communicators require two traits:

1. The ability to accept that all emotions coexist within their hearts and, when appropriate, the willingness to share them
2. A belief that people we talk with have a complete range of emotions and that any one particular emotion doesn't represent their entire being

Do you share your full self when speaking? A few questions to determine if you are a successful communicator:

*   Do conversations generally lead to negative outcomes?
*   Do you fail to get what you want in life?
*   Are career goals hindered by being too weak or too strong?
*   Are people turned off by your speaking or lack of it?

- Do you struggle asking and telling?
- Do emotions get in the way when talking?
- Are relationships a struggle, leaving a sense of hopelessness or frustration?
- Does your silence confuse people?
- Do you lack confidence when speaking?

More yes than no answers says that you have work to do. These questions involve balance, the ability to maintain a sense of equilibrium when talking. If your answers reveal a life lacking balance then this guide can provide a path to understanding.

So how do you achieve the balance of a strong river where talking, listening and all emotions flow together?

Yinyang

An oral English teacher in a foreign country enjoys the wonderful opportunity to learn as much as the students.

My five years teaching at Jianghan University helped me to understand the importance the Chinese place on balance and acceptance. Chinese philosophy embraces the belief that life's opposite emotions don't compete but complement.

The philosophy, known as yinyang, involves the idea that life elements compete with AND complement each other.

Flip a coin. Heads or tails may win. But regardless of the victor, it is still one coin. Emotions, such as weak and strong, kind and greedy, or talkative and quiet, exist the same way. Flip your emotions but they are still one coin.

TOP TIP
EMOTIONS COMPLEMENT ONE ANOTHER.
COULD YOU BE HAPPY IF YOU DIDN'T KNOW SAD?

The terms yin and yang cannot be separately used. The Chinese say this is not possible because a one-sided coin does not exist any more than a happy person. Sadness lives with happiness.

Weak and strong occur as a single continuum that includes everything from the very strong to the very weak. The force interacts to form a dynamic system in which the whole is greater than the assembled parts.

Yinyang combines opposite thoughts with the yin character defined as the dark or cloudy side of the hill while yang the bright or sunny side. Many Chinese words combine two thoughts (characters) so two concepts blend into one idea.

Let's look at the example of a push and pull door. Push a door open to its fullest extent and it immediately goes back into the pull quality. A retreat follows every advance. Push needs pull or no door exists!

The yinyang of talking involves a similar range of textures, feelings, and emotions. The dark brings brooding, angry words, stopping conversations, instilling fear, and chilling the air. The light brings bright, comforting words, stimulating conversation, exciting people, and encouraging life and growth.

A wide range of dark and light conversations make up a person's life. Understanding yinyang allows acceptance of any conversation for what it is, the stream of life.

Do you incorporate a full range of emotion when talking or do you speak English like the pull part of a push-pull door? Always in retreat, pulling back from the conveying of ideas and opinions? The push part does live within you.

Seeking Balance's goal is for you to understand and accept all emotions, thoughts and ideas. Yinyang allows for the person's strong yang side (fast, hard, solid, and focused) to live in peace with the soft yin side (kind and yielding).

Every person's spirit and speaking skills contain both qualities.

Yin is defined as feminine, black, dark, north, water (transformation), passive, moon, earth, cold, old, even numbers, valleys, poor, soft, and provides spirit to all things.

Yang is masculine, white, light, south, fire (creativity), active, sun, heaven, warm, young, odd numbers, mountains, rich, hard, and provides form to all things.

Essentially, yinyang conveys the complicated dualities of life and the paramount need for balance and moderation.

The blind natural law of the universe contains conflicting ideas that also complement. Consider these two thoughts:

- Gravity's consistent force creates constant change to our lives. How can something be both ever consistent and ever changing?
- The Big Bang Theory says the universe can be both a tiny speck of energy and infinite space. How can something be a tiny speck and infinite?

Speaking English contains the same conflicting yet complementary forces, like the peaceful yet powerful river. A person improves their range of emotion and communication skill by embracing both sides of the coin, understanding and accepting that emotions both conflict and complement.

Unlike the river, do you see yourself as peaceful but not powerful? Do you fail to accept your strength? Or do you rage on without accepting your peaceful nature?

Seeking Balance wants you to find a sense of yinyang—an ability to accept all emotions—as a speaker.

"Be aware of the process, consistency and stability set the tone for change and success."

The Nine Tests of Balance

Researchers hypothesize that humans began speaking approximately two million years ago. Evolution improved the ability to talk but challenges still exist for everyone, so don't be disappointed if you still struggle speaking English after a couple decades!

View yourself as a world-class athlete when taking on the challenges of improved English speaking. When an Olympic competitor begins to train, they attack the hurdles before them. They don't shy away from the task but give in to it. The English speaker is no different. When tackling speaking issues, knowing the hurdles beforehand prepares the mind for excellence.

Speaking struggles start with the inability to handle emotions. Incorporating the concept of yinyang into your training allows for the acceptance of a wider range of emotions when communicating. Coming to grips with emotions grounds you, providing a base.

The ability to accept nervousness, that "both calm and anxiety exist within me" allows for balance.

To examine how well you're grounded, *Seeking Balance* provides The Nine Tests of Balance. The exam determines your balance on life's larger issues through the use of English.

How you handle these hurdles provides perspective on everyday conversation with others, providing insights on the way you talk.

Read the short passages and take a few minutes to think about each one. Talk about them with a friend to gain even greater insight.

Where do you stand when it comes to these issues? Do you allow yourself to understand, feel, and communicate both sides of the coin?

1. You and the universe

Every human being wonders how they fit into the universe. Questions such as: "Where did I come from?" "How did the universe start?" and "What happens after I die?" confound us all.

The questions evolved along with the ability to speak over hundreds of thousands of years. Enlightened Chinese, Greek, and Roman philosophers, artists, writers, and musicians thought, spoke, and sang about issues bigger than eating, sleeping, and staying safe.

Freethinkers force us to wonder "How and where do I fit into the silent emptiness of the infinite universe?"

Maybe in the end we are all but a grain of sand on an endless beach or all powerful. Or both! We don't know.

The ability to think, talk, and yet, be a grain of sand on the universe's silent and endless beach seems to be about as contradictory as life gets.

"We are part of this universe; we are in this universe, but perhaps more important than both of those facts, is that the universe is in us."

Neil deGrasse Tyson

But today is all we have and, hopefully, your unique voice rings out thoughts and feelings. Do you shout, talk or whisper every day in your truly special voice that you're alive and want to be heard? If not, then why not?

Ask these questions to check your balance within the universe:

• How do the universe and my voice complement one another in life?
• Am I in balance with the universe or does it frighten me?
• Can I get outside of daily concerns to understand my place in the universe?
• How do my words and actions reflect the bigger picture of life?

Yes, balancing a unique voice in an infinite universe that blows us around like an autumn leaf in a November storm makes life difficult but not impossible.

Start by accepting the universal duality of life. Yinyang shows us the way by describing how seemingly opposite or contrary forces not only help one another but actually need one another to be complete.

To understand the balance between our individual voice and the infinite universe requires a lifetime of reflection. But by grasping the huge difference between the self and the universe then we begin to accept competing emotions. In the end, it's the same concept.

2. Instinct versus emotion

Lao Tzu wrote in *Tao Te Ching* (*The Book of the Way*) that if you're not afraid of dying then there is nothing you can't achieve.

Now this simple statement challenges us all in life. Instincts tell us to avoid dangerous activities that can result in injury or death while emotions implore us to "take that risk, you can do it."

Lao's excellent point involves balancing self-preservation instincts with risk-taking emotions. Our speaking lives revolve around this same dilemma.

A yinyang relationship exists between the brain and speech, much like the push/pull door. We deal with situations where the brain says beware, only to hear our voice say, "Sure, I'll do it." And we do it!

The hardwired brain deals in evolutionary instincts when facing fear, pain or hunger. Instinctual thought demands us to run or fight when fear strikes, eat when hungry, and protect when hurt.

The emotional side takes over when speaking. Instead of hard and fast instinctual answers, we get either indecisive, weak words and actions or irrational responses based on emotion.

Yes, clarity between thought, words and action create daily dilemmas. It's hard to know why we say or do anything.

Our brain and what we say appear to be complementary but conflicting forces. The brain, instinctual and finely developed through millions of years of evolution, battles with spoken English which uses modern-day experiences and desires.

The world-famous Mayo Clinic says this regarding how the brain operates:

"Your brain contains billions of nerve cells arranged in patterns that coordinate thought, emotion, behavior, movement and sensation. A complicated highway system of nerves connects your brain to the rest of your body, so communication can occur in split seconds. Think about how fast you pull your hand back from a hot stove. While all the parts of your brain work together, each part is responsible for a specific function—controlling everything from your heart rate to your mood."

The Mayo Clinic says the brain coordinates and works together with other parts of the body. The brain coordinates the body as best it can. But each part acts independently of the brain, explaining why the instinctual brain and emotional mouth aren't always on the same wavelength!

So while the brain communicates with a person's spoken English center, it doesn't control it. The brain acts like an air traffic control tower while speaking ability is the jet taking off. The control tower sends directions, pointing out danger but the pilot makes the final call.

How many times a week do you say or think, "I don't know why I said that?" Or, "Why did I do that?"

I do all the time. I've concluded that the instinctual brain and the emotional mouth are independent of one another. The two live apart, the instinctual brain giving orders while emotional words and actions are regularly going rogue.

"Poetry is not a turning loose of emotion, but an escape from emotion; it is not the expression of personality but the escape from personality. But, of course, only those who have emotions and personality know what it means to want to escape from these things."

T.S. Eliot

Accepting the yinyang relationship encourages balance between thought, emotion, and action. Both instincts and emotions drive us. Problems occur when these functions aren't in sync and one takes over leaving us "out of control."

Keep these questions in mind when instincts and emotions battle:

- Do my emotional words create imbalance?
- My instincts keep me safe but do I neglect or bury my emotions?
- Should I just keep quiet until I can sort out my emotions?

3. True and false

What is true and what is false? The world struggles with this question more than ever before. Today's black-and-white media world creates narratives that use screaming headlines to espouse the "truth" in stories that end up misleading at best.

Let's look at true and false from a yinyang perspective where both exist on one spectrum, leaving few things absolutely true or false.

If true/false is like a push/pull door then once the door reaches absolute truth, it begins to immediately swing back to the false.

Conversations contain this element when a person isn't satisfied giving the simple truth but tries to push farther causing overstatements, bluster, or falsehoods. The door swings back to the false.

TOP TIP
BOTH TRUE AND FALSE PLAY A PART IN ALL LIVES.
THEY ARE INSEPARABLE.

Individuals live along the same spectrum of the true self versus false self. What would you consider true or false in how you live? Do you hide true feelings or opinions, making a false life easier? Do you dye your hair or wear slimming spandex clothes? Does hiding the truth make life better?

Take comfort in the knowledge that yinyang sees true and false as one. One cannot exist without the other. No one lives a total true or false life. But acknowledging the existence of falseness in life starts the process of reflection.

"A hair divides what is false and true."
Omar Khayyam

Listen carefully to the words that come out of your mouth ringing with false intentions, driven by insecurity, potential personal gain, fear, or bravado. A yinyang perspective keeps the true and false life in balance when speaking.

4. Known and unknown

How many conversations seem as if you're driving home on a foggy night? Where the discussion feels like a familiar place coming out of the fog only to disappear into a haze of blinding darkness? Did we hear something we recognize or not?

Balancing what we know and don't know in conversation takes an ability to keep an open mind. Conversations get derailed because people think they know the context when they really don't. True wisdom comes from stepping back and admitting ignorance.

Context: The circumstances that form the setting for an event, statement, or idea, and in terms of which it can be fully understood and assessed.

No conversation is fully understood without knowing the context. Why am I saying these words and why are you saying those words? Failing to understand the context creates imbalance and distress.

An example:

A young boy and girl wait at a bus stop. They don't know each other. The boy asks the girl, "Do you know if this bus is late?" She replies, "I am not sure. Hopefully it will be here soon."

The simple question and answer cause a myriad of thoughts to occur in both parties.

The girl wonders about the question's context. She may think:

a) Is he late for an important meeting or just impatient?
b) Does he think I'm attractive and want to start a conversation?
c) Is he trying to find out if I regularly take this bus?
d) Is he a new bus rider and unsure of himself?
e) Is he dangerous?

The boy listens to the girl's answer and wonders:

a) Did the question make her nervous because she doesn't know me?
b) Is she a new bus rider?
c) Does she think I'm handsome and wants to encourage me?
d) Is she preoccupied with her own issues?
e) Does she think I'm a loser for riding the bus?

The lack of context in the simple conversation causes distress. Instead of listening with an open, unprejudiced mind the boy and girl create their own context by imagining what the other person is thinking.

TOP TIP
PROPER CONTEXT REQUIRES KNOWLEDGE NOT GUESSES.

Too often our minds make up scenarios that have nothing to do with reality. We tell ourselves things like, "Oh he must hate me because my hair looks awful today" or "My boss thinks I'm a slacker for being five minutes late." How do you really know unless you ask?

Which side of the coin do you fall on when coming to unsubstantiated conclusions? Are you suspicious or anxious by jumping to conclusions? Or do you believe everything at face value and place no judgment on the conversation until the true context reveals itself?

Maintain balance and reduce distress by keeping an open mind regarding what you know and don't know. When in doubt, ask.

5. Hard and soft

Hard and soft create a powerful yinyang dynamic. Maintaining a proper balance within the force takes effort.

Situations arise in life which require a strong position when speaking. Standing up for a clean environment, against physical abuse, or for world peace takes a committed, clear voice.

"Life is like riding a bicycle. To keep your balance, you must keep riding."

Albert Einstein

But other times intimidation or fear makes passive speakers. A ranting boss, angry customer, or strict police officer forces us to respond in a quiet, respectful, but submissive tone.

Personalities play a key role in these situations. A super aggressive man decides to yell back at a ranting boss only to lose his job. A shy girl ignores speaking out against physical abuse, which only leads to more abuse. An angry man gets arrested for screaming at a police officer.

Handling a situation takes tact. A great leader is both warrior and healer, allowing things to happen and shaping them as they come. The wise person accepts both sides of the coin, realizing when the soft overcomes the hard like water against the rock and when the powerful, unwavering voice is required.

Being too hard or too soft creates imbalance. Where do your problems lie when it comes to this dynamic? Are you too soft or too hard?

6. Humans and machines

The yinyang relationship between humans and machines creates a modern-day balancing act.

The reality of an increasingly technological world hits us every day. The now-ubiquitous, head-down pose of the smartphone user sneaking a glance at Facebook, WeChat, or Twitter makes human conversation difficult.

Potentially entertaining conversations or gorgeous sunsets lose to the siren call of funny cat videos, sports updates, video games, movie star gossip, and shopping sites.

Smartphones and social media allow us to positively manipulate our lives in a multitude of ways, but are as addictively unfulfilling as a bowl of potato chips.

TOP TIP
EXCESSIVE SOCIAL MEDIA USE HAS BEEN LINKED TO DEPRESSION, ANXIETY, FEELINGS OF LONELINESS AND ISOLATION, AND LOWER SELF-ESTEEM.

Studies suggest four warning signs for cellphone addiction: a) It continually gets in the way of working, b) You can't voluntarily stop, c) It's the most important thing in your life and, d) You feel bad when you can't use it.

Technology obsession speaks to the philosophy that the more you have the less secure you feel. Along with money, guns, power, and social media contacts, technology creates the driving sensation of "I don't have enough. I feel insecure so I need more."

But more doesn't bring happiness. A smartphone never hires anyone for a great job, eats dinner with you, goes out on a date, or brings you a birthday present. Balance requires accepting the smartphone IMPROVES your life but is NOT your life.

Why have 800 Facebook contacts if you never see, laugh, or have a cup of coffee with them?

Speaking to another human is scary stuff. Risk of failure, embarrassment, ignorance, and disappointment lurk in the weeds along the path to conversation.

Successfully balancing the allure and safety of technology and digital friends with actual human contact and conversation creates the perfect modern-day life.

Do you do both in a proper balance? Have you attained equilibrium between you and your machines?

"All the stress, suffering and addiction come from not realizing you already are what you are looking for."
Jon Kabat-Zinn

7. Us and them

The rock star of international language is English. Close to two billion people now speak English. Nothing comes close to spoken English's ability to change the world through its reach, financial value, and power.

- The world's business, education, and entertainment run through the English language. Travel the world, go to an Asian or European movie theater or watch international news to see the tremendous influence English holds.
- The language dominates newspaper publishing, book publishing, international telecommunications, scientific publishing, international trade, mass entertainment, and diplomacy.

- High-powered occupations like medicine and computing require a working knowledge of English.
- More than 80 percent of the world's scientific journals are published in English.
- Most heads of state, international business leaders, and top educators speak English. News broadcasts and newspapers spread the language to all corners of the world.

Nothing shows the value of English more than the fact that non-native English speakers now outnumber native speakers three to one. English speakers living in a non-English-speaking country understand the language's influence throughout the world.

English's importance on a world stage filters down to you. People who want to succeed internationally or locally (whether that's Beijing, Brussels, or Boston) need to command English like a well-trained dog fetching the right English word as if it were a bone.

Americans remain blasé regarding English's growing importance in world politics and business. Americans spend $100 billion a year on losing weight and another $100 billion on cosmetics. They believe thin and pretty bring success not the English language.

The rest of the world disagrees, viewing English as the road to attainment. The Chinese spend billions to improve English skills as do people in India, the Middle East, Russia, and Europe. They see English as a valuable tool that brings success.

Worldwide competition to speak English has never been greater because its influence has never been greater. The language's superstar status requires speaking excellence regardless of whether English is your first, second, or tenth language.

In your lifetime chances are you will do business, teach, or interact with someone from another culture, most likely American, Chinese, Indian,

Middle Eastern, or Russian. The transaction will likely take place in English. Will you be able to hold your own in that conversation?

English-as-a-first-language (EFL) speakers regard this as a no-brainer, thinking, "An ESL (English-as-a-second-language) speaker can't hold a candle to my native-born talents."

The overconfident native speaker needs to watch their wallet! Many ESL speakers work tirelessly on improving English language skills. They understand from the steady drumbeat of their culture that improving English skills increases the chances of success.

ESLers work at improving English skills more than EFLers (English as a first language). Why? ESLers strive to improve because they see themselves as the underdog, trying to win in a game run by native English speakers. Nothing gives them more pride than besting a native English speaker.

Native and non-native speakers alike need to accept the reality that the hyper-competitive world economy runs on English. The chance to succeed in creating or selling ideas, products, or services in the future requires the ability to use the English language as a trusted and highly competent friend.

Balance requires understanding that English dominates the world of business and commerce but is not the exclusive domain of any one country. English remains throughout the world an equal-opportunity language.

Great athletes want to compete against top competitors. In the English-speaking economy that means great communicators come from all countries in the world. Achieve balance by respecting all English speakers as equal partners or competitors.

8. Winning and losing

This balance test involves the complicated consideration of winning and losing. The sports-crazy world rotates on the idea of who is ahead or behind like a World Cup match.

The winning and losing dynamic plays out on the Internet, which pits one side against another by using screaming, divisive headlines declaring a daily knockout winner.

This competitive environment makes us lose sight of an earlier stated fact: English speaking is not a zero-sum game.

Speaking to another person allows for the exchange of information, emotions, opinions, and knowledge. The "losing" side gains benefit even in one-sided conversations.

Conversations do produce short-term winners and losers. But by viewing the outcome through yinyang, we realize winning and losing live on the same continuum. One cannot exist without the other. Today's winners become tomorrow's losers. Today's losers may come out on top tomorrow.

Balance asks to keep every conversation in perspective. Don't get too excited if the conversation goes well or off the cliff. It is only one conversation in a lifetime full of opportunities. True winners realize another game starts soon.

To maintain equilibrium, keep strong values, listen, connect with others, contribute to society, assume responsibility, remain optimistic, and know your strengths and flaws. Don't hold onto one victory as proof of success. View yourself not as a winner or loser but as a competitor who continues to work toward excellence throughout life.

Top-notch athletes live in the moment, blocking out yesterday's defeats and victories. They start each match, each game, each day with the idea that the score is 0-0. Only now matters.

TOP TIP
EVERYONE LOSES. NOT EVERYONE'S A LOSER.

Speaking requires the same tenacity. Do your best today. Learn from mistakes, but don't define yourself by them. Everyone loses but that doesn't make everyone a loser. Balance teaches us that yesterday's win or loss means nothing today.

This book does not view language as a tool to conquer but a bridge-building tool to the future. Speak English not as a winner or loser but as a friend of the world.

9. Open or closed?

The final test involves whether words and actions leave you open or closed.

Open: Allowing access, passage, or a view through an empty space; not closed or blocked up.

Closed: Having boundaries; enclosed; blocked or barred to passage or entry.

Words show our true state in life with respect to being open or closed. Words can liberate or keep us in bondage.

An open English speaker mimics the world-class athlete by being prepared for all potential situations. Balance allows them to keep an open mind and react, revealing a powerful yinyang dynamic at work.

Do you see the potential of every conversation, or are you closed-off in a world of conditioned responses, a prison built by words?

An example:

Bob asks Mary to a party. He says that she won't know anyone at the party but that the people are friendly. He mentions that one of the guests owns a company and is looking for a person with her skills. He says it's a great opportunity since Mary needs a new job.

But Mary believes she's shy, and meeting new people makes her nervous. She tells Bob what she always says in these situations, "I'd love to go, Bob, but I'm busy," and she sits home alone once more.

Does this sound familiar? Do repetitive responses keep you caged, stopping life experiences and the potential of positive growth?

Many face life like Mary, living with a "fear of the unknown." Should we be more afraid of the known or the unknown? Should we be more afraid of what we always say or what we don't know?

Conditioned responses create boundaries that prevent true freedom and growth, stopping us before the chance to experience true potential.

We believe the words keep us safe, but the question we don't ask is: "Safe from what?" Too often well-rehearsed words prevent exploration of a richer, more varied existence.

Seeking Balance wants you to examine your words. Have you constructed a personal prison, built word by word from conditioned responses?

Are you open or closed?

Conclusion

The Nine Tests of Balance determine your view of the world. Can you see existence in a yinyang frame of mind? Grasping and accepting the entire range of thought and emotion in each of the tests?

The tests' results play a role in how you communicate with others. Accepting or denying the emotions involved in these nine topics determine balance as an English speaker.

"Dig the well before you are thirsty."

SECTION TWO

CHANGE

THE CONSCIOUS ACT OF BECOMING DIFFERENT

Mindfulness: The road to change

"Like a dream that a person struggles to recall but has nothing but a dim sense of beauty until that fades, leaving the dreamer to bitterly accept the old hard waking and all its penalties."

Kenneth Grahame, *The Wind in the Willows*

THE INABILITY TO SPEAK FREELY leaves the sense of despair described in Kenneth Grahame's beautiful paragraph. Dreams of well-spoken words live inside but too often fade into the dismal existence of silence.

How can dreams become reality? How can change take place in life to allow the real you to emerge?

Personal change requires developing new habits. This section looks at effective but achievable ways to change behaviors that prevent communicating.

Start by focusing on what you do now. Too often, we ignore negative actions, rationalizing or denying their existence or impact. The road to change begins with awareness.

People who diet monitor calories and fat content in the foods they eat. This allows for calculation of the impact of an apple versus a piece of cheesecake.

Try an experiment by observing everything you say for two or three days. Listen to every word and take time to give full attention to what and why the words came out of your mouth. Try to get in touch with the full range of emotion that the situation creates within you.

You may be sad but say something happy. You may want to comment but remain silent. Be mindful of the conflicting but complementary emotions. Don't judge them but just acknowledge their existence.

Hopefully, you'll begin to accept a wider range of emotions that allows more creative thought to come to the surface. Accessing more honest emotions allows for better conversation.

Be mindful of your full range of complementary but conflicting emotions. Acknowledge the sunny side of the mountain as well as the shady side.

Negative thoughts

Communication stops for many reasons. A speaker's poor balance contributes to most conversation breakdowns.

Let's look at an example.

Jack, an employee, talks to his boss, Judy. This makes him nervous since he always fears bad news. The negative thoughts due to fear and self-doubt make Jack feel as if he's being spun round and round until dizzy. Judy just wants to update him on a new plan but unsteady Jack loses balance in the conversation, preventing communicating with a clear mind. He says confusing things making Judy shake her head in disbelief while walking away from him. Jack created a problem where none existed.

Seven negative or disempowering thoughts stop conversations before they begin. Change starts with stopping these feelings:

1. **SELF-DEFEATING TALK:** People fail before starting because they continually think or say things such as "I can't do it," "I'm not good enough," or "I know I'm going to fail." Give yourself a chance by saying "I can do this" or, at least, "I'm going to do my best."

2. **COMPARISONS:** Comparing yourself to others guarantees stress, anxiety, and depression. Others will always be richer, smarter, and better looking. If you know you have enough, then you are truly rich. Seek excellence not success.

3. **THE PAST:** Dwelling over a negative past solves nothing. Yes, it is difficult to let go, but all you have is today. If your words are about yesterday, then you've missed today's boat to a better life.

4. **PEOPLE WHO STEAL YOUR POWER:** Letting others disempower through manipulation, bullying, fear, or anger makes you a victim. They take your strength, making your words reactive and weak. Balance can never be achieved in this situation.

5. **THE BLAME GAME:** Once the blaming starts, it never ends. Blaming others for misfortunes makes you the victim. The blamed may deserve it, but holding others responsible only makes your words bitter, resentful, and powerless. The blamed don't know or don't care so your words never lead to happiness, good health, or success.

6. **SELF-FORGIVENESS:** Being self-compassionate is difficult. We beat ourselves up for mistakes we make, refusing to forgive and forget. The best advice is to do your best and then let go.

7. **SEEKING PERFECTION:** The fear of failure comes with feeling you're not good enough. Putting undue pressure on yourself to be perfect leads to unhappiness because no one is perfect, including you. Accept who you are, warts and all.

Seeking Balance's central theme encourages equilibrium while talking. These seven negative or disempowering thoughts make communicating seem like you're fighting a seven-headed monster.

"Those who see through the fear will always be safe."

Accepting change into your life

If unsteadiness prevents the conveying of ideas and opinions to others, then the time is right to seek balance. This starts by accepting the challenge to change.

Don't cling to the comfort of thinking that all is well. Give in to the challenges by accepting these ideas:

- All people struggle. It's healthy to acknowledge it.
- Learn to unlearn bad habits.
- Start listening to your true voice.
- Adopt the philosophy that nothing changes until you do.
- Stop blaming because, once started, blaming never stops.
- Accept yourself and the world accepts you.

Threefold training

Buddhists use Threefold Training to change the mind's thinking and habits.

Threefold Training involves guiding the mind, body, and spirit. Each element plays a key role in the English speaker's ability to change and build balance.

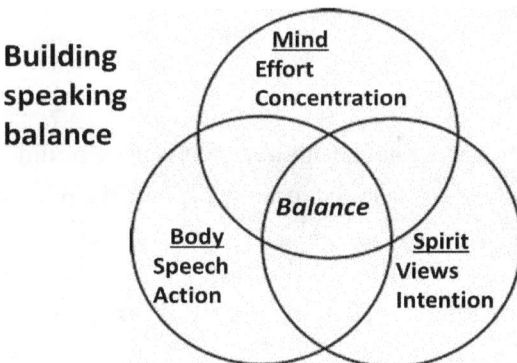

Building speaking balance

Mind
Effort
Concentration

Balance

Body
Speech
Action

Spirit
Views
Intention

Consider these three areas in building balance as a speaker:

1. **MIND**: Properly training the mind involves building sufficient levels of effort and concentration. Excellence in any endeavor requires focus. The chances for improvement skyrockets when focusing on the details necessary for positive outcomes.
2. **BODY:** The body produces speech and action. Excellent speech requires clear diction, proper volume, appropriate gestures, and pleasing body language. This requires a positive self-image. Change begins when you feel worthy. See yourself as a speaker, not just one who speaks. Concentrate on what your body does while communicating. Train to improve it.
3. **SPIRIT:** The third area involves your true spirit and the subtle ways you communicate. Examine personal views and intentions regarding speech for legitimacy. What are your opinions? Why do you have them? Do they make sense? Do intentions seem valid or selfish? This challenging examination gets to the core of personal intentions. Change what is not consistent with your true spirit.

Bringing these three areas together develops balance as a speaker. Effort, body language, and intentions create a total speaking package.

Effort

Effort determines excellence. Talent helps but effort makes the difference. The hardest workers, not the most talented, usually become the most successful.

- J.K. Rowling, the author of the *Harry Potter* series, was broke and began writing her series on the back of napkins on the daily train to London.

- Inventor Thomas Edison failed 2,000 times before discovering the light bulb.
- Billionaire Jack Ma, China's richest man, rode 70 miles a day on his bicycle as a youth to give tourists tours so he could practice English. He did this for nine years.

"When you're not practicing, someone else is getting better."

NBA star Allen Iverson

Being excellent at playing ping-pong, singing, cooking, writing, or speaking in English comes with preparation. Developing a skill takes nothing but time and effort.

Improvement starts by setting a regular time and place. Good times to practice communication skills may be the first or last thing you do each day. Or take Jack Ma's idea by getting a job that requires speaking.

Practicing does not have to be long. Fifteen minutes a day produces noticeable results over time.

Research shows two important points to keep in mind when practicing.

1. Don't practice for endless hours
2. Move around while practicing

Long cramming sessions lose effectiveness. Shorter periods of study work better. Also, don't sit in a bedroom or small room. Get out and move around. Physical stimulation awakens the brain, allowing for the retention of information.

The Chinese student's daily pledge

In 2015, I taught 12-year-old students at an oral English camp in Jingman, China, a delightful group of bright, hardworking students.

Each day they recited a pledge to do their best to learn English. The promise served as a daily reminder to pursue excellence.

Speak...Speak...Speak

I don't care about how badly or how well I speak; I only care about catching the chance to speak. I don't care about what other people think; I only care about making progress. The more I speak, the better my English will be.

The more mistakes I make, the more progress I will make. I must enjoy making mistakes. I must enjoy speaking English.

Practice makes perfect, so I won't be shy, I will try my best. I will make it. I will do it. I believe!

The right attitude starts with training the mind to believe.

Look in the refrigerator

Mindfulness: A mental state achieved by focusing one's awareness on the present moment, while calmly acknowledging and accepting one's feelings, thoughts, and bodily sensations.

Mindfulness transcends shyness, nervousness, arrogance, intimidation, and fear. Mindfulness means accepting all that the moment holds.

"With mindfulness, you can establish yourself in the present in order to touch the wonders of life that are available in that moment."

Nhat Hanh

The road to change starts with being mindful. The communication process works best when calmly accepting the results that come with your words and actions.

The wheels to personal change start rolling once you become aware.

Self-awareness and acceptance is like knowing the food in your refrigerator before starting to cook. The question becomes a simple one: "I know what I have. What can I do with it?"

TOP TIP
MINDFULNESS LEADS TO CHANGE.

Here is my story of awareness and acceptance.

My personal struggles lasted a number of years. My career was quite successful up until 2008. I had made a lot of money but it wasn't enough. I began to mistakenly believe that the normal working world was beneath me.

My earlier success led me to start chasing unrealistic dreams with a decided lack of discipline. I bounced back and forth between starting new poorly planned businesses and writing the great American novel.

Haphazard effort caused business ideas as well as attempts at writing to go up in flames. My bank account spiraled downward.

Excuses for poor results were always available. I blamed the ideas, a lack of time, other people, a cruel world, the weather and any other convenient reason. The truth was I was waiting for a miracle to happen.

I blew through a lot of money in a few years. Desperation rose as my bank account sank. I needed a job. Stumbling through the Internet one day, an ad popped up looking for English teachers in China.

I had a degree in education and had been a teacher for a few years fresh out of college. To sink back to teaching after numerous career successes seemed utterly depressing, but what choice did I have?

With my ego-infused "hero" plans dead, I became an ordinary spoken-English teacher in a foreign country. Not a talented novelist. Not a brilliant businessman. I was a simple teacher getting below minimum wages.

TOP TIP
CHANGE IS LIBERATING.

Much to my surprise, the move to China shook me loose from my downward spiral. Soon positive days began to stack up. I enjoyed the job and students liked me. My unrealistic dreams faded along with my stress. My attention on teaching spoken English became sharper.

I began to think about how to teach oral English. *My focus shifted from me to my students. I wanted to be an excellent teacher so I could help other human beings.*

TOP TIP
JUST DO SOMETHING.

I realized that success didn't matter because I was doing what made use of my limited talents. I finally understood what people meant when they say "it's the process that's fun, not the success."

Change in life begins when you look in the refrigerator and see what you have to cook. Dwell in reality by accepting who you are and working toward excellence. Set goals and get to work.

Start putting the right ingredients together

Self-help book readers want positive influences in their world. You want to be a better English speaker and this book helps. That's a great start.

Now it's time to begin putting the right ingredients together to make a better you.

Open your "refrigerator" and see what's inside. Don't be judgmental or disappointed. Great things come from surprising mixtures of ingredients. The world's greatest dishes usually come from the combination of two or more ingredients thought incompatible.

Maybe your refrigerator has a can of shyness, a package of self-doubt and a bunch of dried-up confidence hidden in the back. No worries! Let's see what we can stir up.

TOP TIP
DON'T BE AFRAID OF GROWING SLOWLY, BE AFRAID OF STANDING STILL.

The right techniques

A world-class chef uses well-established cooking and baking methods to produce culinary magic. Learning to speak English well is no different. Add a few excellent techniques and watch your speaking improve.

Technique: A skillful or efficient way of doing or achieving something.

Technique 1: Learn to unlearn

Everyone flirts with eloquence. We all utter a poetic phrase, witty retort, or insightful observation from time to time. But like the dreamer, the brilliance of the moment fades, leaving the sad acceptance of a limited speaking skill.

Stop for a moment. Why accept mediocrity? Start creating daily magical moments. How? Realize you're not perfect and work for positive change. Many successful people have said "it took me years of work to be an overnight sensation."

The world needs you. It is filled with too many proud and stupid toads that do little more than croak. A critical shortage of thoughtful, strong speakers exists and we need your magic.

How to start? Easy! The road to change starts with unlearning. Forget the harmful habits and dogmatic principles that trap you in prison and open up to opportunity.

I moved to China and broke the chains of my prison. What can you do to escape the memorized words, actions, or thoughts that stop you from real change?

Habitual conversation makes us like trained seals balancing a ball on our nose and barking to entertain the crowd. Our trainer asks a question, we bark and he throws us a fish. We unflinchingly know our lines.

Maybe you *think* you're smart as a whip or dumb as a doornail; shy like a flittering butterfly or aggressive and overbearing as a telephone sales-person. The world bakes an image into us like apples in a pie. We've been told and we've retold ourselves so many times who we are that we can't tell the apples from the pie.

This unfortunate circumstance stops the ability to experience your full range of emotion and thought. Shyness may exist within you, but so does vivaciousness. So much more lives within you.

Did you ever make a conscious decision to "be" this person known as you? Or did parents, teachers, friends, and a misguided child (you) lead you to a place where only a part of you now exists?

Stop being a circus act, learn to unlearn. Be mindful that much more of you exists. Let it come out.

Technique 2: Relax and listen

What's harder: Learning or unlearning how to tie your shoes? Unlearning routine can be very hard. You want to change bad habits but how in the heck do you do it when the body goes into automatic pilot?

Change comes slowly and only after resolving personal challenges. Relax if you don't understand.

The key to change doesn't involve high activity, numerous promises, and vows to perform days of intensive training or a Spartan diet.

TOP TIP
TRANSFORMATION REQUIRES STOPPING AND LISTENING.
BE STILL AS A CAT — CALM, QUIET, AND
AWARE OF THE SURROUNDINGS.

"It is not the strongest of the species that survives, nor the most intelligent, but the one most responsive to change."

Charles Darwin

Change requires being quiet enough to hear the answer when it comes.

Today's society wants instant gratification. We want change NOW. Maybe you're reading this book because of an embarrassing event or an opportunity for success presents itself. You need help ASAP.

Sorry, this book contains no miracles. Expecting immediate results lacks stability, leading to bad decisions and disappointment. Excellence comes by quietly listening for the answer and then doing the work.

"Nothing will work unless you do."

John Wooden, Hall of Fame coach

Technique 3: Being not doing

Great athletes talk about "being in the zone" where athletic perfection goes through the body unimpeded by thought. The game flows through them like a mystical river where excellence comes in every movement.

This type of confidence goes beyond the self-assurance of ability. The person transforms from doing to being. He or she not only can do it but is it.

Lao's book told readers about the importance of "being not doing." A person *is* confident, he doesn't *do* confident. Stop trying to do things. Be confident in who you are, let go, and let things happen.

Nike, the multinational company, branded itself with the unforgettable phrase, "Just do it." Have they misled the world? Using Lao's idea, the famous Nike slogan should be "Just be it" not "Just do it."

Mindfulness and practice not wishing and hoping create confidence. A mindful person who practices guitar, singing or shooting a basketball sees themselves as a guitarist, singer or player. They don't do it, they are it. They become the music or the ball.

An audience watching a wonderful dancer cannot separate the dance from the dancer, they are one. What separates the painting from the painter?

You may work as a grocery store clerk while going to law school at night. What do you do and who are you? Are you a clerk who likes to study law or a future attorney who works as a clerk?

Speaking English is the same. Effort, visualizing who you are, letting things happen and simply being transforms a person from being one who speaks to a speaker.

TOP TIP
VISUALIZE SUCCESS.

Each of us must decide who we are, our being. What's in our own refrigerator?

Don't think that doing makes you a being! Giving a speech at work or school doesn't make you a powerful speaker. Only working toward excellence does.

Know the difference between being and doing by looking into your heart! Accept your true being and try to improve it. Don't let others tell you who you are.

Technique 4: Get it together

Unfortunately, putting in the necessary work to improve eludes many people. The fourth challenge to change requires getting your life together.

The phrase "get it together" has been in American pop culture for decades. It means to reflect on shortcomings and change. This involves refocusing by letting go of harmful ways and coming back to the light.

Here are five ways to "get it together."

1. **BE RECEPTIVE TO NEW THOUGHT**: Stuck in a rut thinking the same old thoughts or doing the same old things? Start looking for new ideas that appeal to you.
2. **START GROWING**: The wise gardener trims away the weak and dead tree branches to allow for new growth. Preserving the "old" prevents growth. Prune to start growing again.
3. **FORWARD NOT BACK**: Don't cling to past successes in life. Yeah, maybe you were smart in 10th grade Algebra or had a good job until they cut the workforce. Ask: "What's next?"
4. **OPEN AGENDA**: Don't stick to the same old agenda. Being a creature of habit is comforting but stops progress. Change your weekly calendar to add time for personal growth.
5. **REALITY**: Dwell in reality by letting illusions go. Stop believing things that aren't true. Be brutally honest. What's real and what's an illusion?

New parents prepare for a new baby by creating a comfortable space in the home by redoing a spare room. View your life like a baby is coming, removing the unnecessary and unproductive and providing the necessary space for the "baby" to flourish.

After getting it together, ask these questions regarding improvement:

- Am I personally prepared and excited to handle growth?
- Do I have what it takes to stick to positive change?

Technique 5: Rejoice in who you are

Some successful people never see themselves as thriving. Doubt and insecurity haunt them even in the face of a fruitful life.

A friend of mine lives in a million-dollar home. She tells everyone how she eats nothing but peanut-butter-and-jelly sandwiches to survive. Her story couldn't be further from the truth.

I finally had to tell her "Stop it. You have a beautiful house, great kids, and a productive job. No one believes your sob story, and I don't know why you think you need to tell it."

Too many of us doubt or question our own success. Ancient philosophy says to rejoice in who you are. If you accept nothing is lacking in life then the whole world opens up. Stop doubting the million-dollar you!

Technique 6: Pursue excellence

What is success? How do you define it? Money? Power? Many friends? Praise from others?

The sixth challenge along the path of change requires you to pursue excellence.

Don't chase success, pursue excellence. Excellence comes from realizing, accepting, and improving skills that enhance your authentic spirit. Money has nothing to do with excellence nor do friends, houses, or nice words from strangers.

TOP TIP
PRAISE WILL NEVER MAKE YOU HAPPY. STOP LOOKING TO OTHERS FOR FULFILLMENT BECAUSE IT GUARANTEES YOU'LL NEVER BE FULFILLED.

A skilled person knows who they are and what they want to achieve, and then does their best to make it happen. Success finds excellence. Accept and improve your true self.

Technique 7: Take it easy

A great piece of English advice that fits countless situations is "take it easy."

Chinese philosophy says, "Things come and she lets them come. Things go and she lets them go." The basic idea is to take it easy.

Attempting to make the world conform to your wishes requires an impossible uphill struggle. If you succeed in forcing others to comply, then the chances anyone will be happy, including you, are slim to none.

The wise individual allows things to happen and shapes them as they come. Being one with nature requires molding life in a genuine way. Barking orders at the soil to work harder doesn't make flowers grow. Wise gardeners simply allow nature to do its thing. No force required.

Trying too hard to achieve something causes the opposite to occur. Keep these points in mind:

- People stop listening when overwhelmed with words
- Students stop learning when the teacher tries too hard
- If you work too hard to be beautiful then you become ugly
- Trying too hard to be kind leads to being overbearing

Do your best and let it go.

Technique 8: Poise under pressure

The eighth technique to change is maintaining poise under pressure.

A person who remains calm when facing challenging situations separates the leaders from the want-to-be leaders.

Poise synonyms: Balance, equilibrium, control, grace, gracefulness, presence.

Failing to maintain poise in a conversation includes becoming too forceful, out of control, imbalanced or frustrated.

Focus on poise as a speaker. Be mindful of how the loss of equilibrium causes a loss of balance, undermining any chance of excellence.

Do you lose poise when:

- Telling others your feelings?
- Meeting new people?
- Expressing emotion?
- Asking questions?
- Talking to strangers?
- Dealing with friends and coworkers?

Trying too hard, losing poise, and falling down hurts. The wise speaker doesn't force things but steps back, lets things come to them and shapes them.

Accept and acknowledge who you are and all your emotions. Be mindful of building a balance between you and your emotions to find a true voice.

The successful implementation of these eight speaking techniques begins the process of meaningful change.

"The key to creating the mental space before responding is mindfulness. Mindfulness is a way of being present; paying attention to and accepting what is happening in our lives. It helps us to be aware of and step away from our automatic and habitual reactions to our everyday experiences."

Elizabeth Thornton

Visualization: A mental rehearsal

The drumbeat of negative messages in our heads stops beneficial transformation. How can you change in the face of these thoughts?

- "I'm not good enough."
- "I can't do it."
- "I'm lazy."
- "I'll never stop (being shy, being a poor speaker, drinking too much, eating too much, being a poor student, etc.)."

Change requires a "can-do" attitude that comes from a positive frame of mind.

A strong, positive self-image is the best possible preparation for excellence. A poor self-image dwells on failures rather than triumphs.

If you hear a constant drumbeat of being unworthy then you're beat before starting. The psychological term is creating a "self-fulfilling prophecy."

Self-fulfilling prophecy: Something that you cause to happen by saying and expecting that it will happen.

The negativity needs to stop. Winners see victory by visualizing success.

Visualization produces a daily vision of personal excellence. Start visioning life as a poised and articulate English speaker and positive changes will begin to emerge.

Instead of slurping from the trough of failure, defeat and broken dreams, visualization allows one to see visions of achievement.

The process involves a mixture of winning imagery and belief. Great athletes and successful individuals use it as a formula for attainment.

Visualization combats doubt and fear by producing a mind-changing ability to "see" the outcome of desired results.

Visualization engrains into a winning psyche the belief in triumph by "seeing" victory without fear or false bravado.

Let's try visualization.

STEP 1: Sit in a comfortable chair, close your eyes, and imagine yourself searching the television for a movie to watch. You come upon a movie with your name in the title, such as "The Life of Jim Smith." Click it on. The first scene involves people talking to you. The conversation with each individual is smashing as you are thoughtful, riveting, intelligent, and funny. Imagine as much detail as possible, such as clothing, facial expressions, body movements, and environment. Imagine your feelings in each scene and recreate that sensation in your body.

STEP 2: See yourself getting up from your chair, opening the television screen, and walking into the movie to play yourself. You are the star of the film, talking with the people in your life in perfect ways. Feel the experience.

"Visualize a world where your cherished dreams come true."

STEP 3: Open up the screen and come out of the movie. Sit back in the chair while the movie still plays. See the television screen miraculously shrink down to a golden chalice filled with a magical drink called Visualization. Gently take the chalice and swallow the brew that is true. Imagine each enchanted drop as a hologram containing a full image of you as an excellent speaker. Each drop speeds through your entire body spreading images of a thriving you. The images flow through your bloodstream, traveling to every inch of your being. Take a deep breath, open your eyes and get on with the day.

The process takes five minutes. Practice this technique daily to see a new you, a confident and well-composed person in any situation.

Progress won't come if the mind sees doubt, fear, and failure. Drinking a daily Visualization cocktail starts the process of excellence. Drink from the golden chalice for one week to see a new you emerge. Here's to you!

"Nothing in life is to be feared, it is only to be understood. Now is the time to understand more so that we may fear less."

Marie Curie

Conclusion

People around the world spend billions of dollars, pounds, euros, and other currencies on attempting to change. Sadly, most never succeed. The pursuit of others' approval rather than striving for personal excellence tops the list for reasons for the failure.

Real lasting change comes from pursuing excellence, being the best you can be. You don't need others to tell you that you put in the work.

Pursue attention by losing a few pounds or getting a new haircut and all say how great you look. But when the pounds return or the hair grows back nothing is said. You had your moment in the sun now it's back to reality. No real change took place.

Success by seeking others' approval never lasts. True change only takes place when you change for you.

This section contains a lot of suggestions on how to change. But if I had to boil it down to one simple word it would be belief.

Change requires:

- Belief you can do it
- Belief that it's good for you
- Belief that the change is about you, not others
- Belief that your work will pay off in tangible benefits

I want to ask you a question: Do you want to improve your spoken English ability for yourself or others? If you answer others then I believe you will fail.

Real change is deeply personal. Excellence comes by focusing on you not how others respond. The drive, the will, the "want to" starts and ends with you. If you take the personal challenge, then excellence will follow.

SECTION THREE

THE BODY AND TALKING

THE PHYSICAL ACT OF SPEAKING

Talking in rhythm

Two graceful dancers glide along the floor in a coordinated movement as if guided by an invisible spirit. One dancer anticipates the other's movement, replying with equal eloquence.

What is the secret to the dance couple's success? They've learned that mastering others is strength, but mastering yourself is true power.

AN EXCELLENT LEADER OR SPEAKER MOVES to the right rhythm. Too much force, pressure, or exertion produces a heavy-handed approach that disrupts the process like a dancer stepping on his partner's toes.

Excellent communicators talk with the same grace and style as world-class dancers, instinctively hearing the beat and moving their body to the rhythm of the conversation.

Top-notch speaking skills require much from the speaker beyond properly pronouncing words. The physical elements of communicating play an important role.

TOP TIP

THE BODY COMMUNICATES THE SPIRIT OF THE MESSAGE. FACE, EYES, HANDS AND BODY TELL A LISTENER AS MUCH AS THE WORDS COMING OUT OF THE MOUTH.

Listeners can "feel" a message through body movements whether it's a nervous twitch, a bashful gaze at the floor, or an angry glare.

Try this test to see the importance of the body in communicating. Turn on the television and mute the sound. Watch any person talk to see if you can tell the general tone of their message. Are they happy, sad, or thoughtful? I believe in almost every circumstance you will be able to tell. Their body tells you all you need to know.

"In character, in manner, in style, in all things, the supreme excellence is simplicity."

Henry Wadsworth Longfellow

Relax and reduce

The basic approach to communication involves more than words. This section examines the physical aspects of speaking. Keep these suggestions in mind when engaging another person. Practice them on a regular basis.

Nervous tension causes speakers to fail in conveying an idea. An anxious person overflows with tension creating physical barriers to communication, such as a trembling voice, erratic movements, or poor eye contact.

Relax what is tense

An active listener determines if a speaker is tense much like a physical therapist massages a body to determine tightness. These seven physical acts require relaxation when speaking.

1. **VOICE TONE:** Voice tone charms or alarms, excites or calms. Realize the power a speaker unleashes when using the right tone. Watch a favorite movie to listen how an actor's voice makes viewers happy, sad, angry, or peaceful much like the music behind the dance. Tension causes a voice to crack, become strident, show anger or whine. Manage tone in challenging conversations. A soothing tone solves many problems.

2. **POSTURE:** A speaker's stance makes a difference in performance. The confident stand tall, with a straight back, shoulders slightly back and head held high while a tense speaker may stand rigid or slump their shoulders. Standing tall and *acting* strong and fearless leads to *being* strong and fearless. Be aware of posture.

3. **ENUNCIATION:** Nervous speakers mumble, talk too fast, or slur words. Good speakers relax, slow down, and carefully pronounce each word. How many times in a day do people ask, "What did you say?" More than once or twice requires attention. Practice by talking at a measured pace while clearly pronouncing each word.

4. **PROPER HAND MOVEMENT:** A talented speaker uses the movement of hands to attract listeners' eyes. These movements improve the chance of listening. Avoid continual or abrupt movements by keeping smooth and graceful. Movement also releases tension while emphasizing key points.

- **Speaking Activity:** Use a mirror to practice physical movements while talking. Notice hand movements, eye contact, and facial expressions. Tie certain points of the talk with certain gestures, such as smiling at a joke or using hand gestures to drive home an important point. Keep the expressions and gestures natural and smooth.

5. **IMPROPER HAND MOVEMENT:** A tense speaker may fall into the bad habit of nervous hand movements such as touching their hair or putting hands in front of or around the mouth or head. The hand distracts listeners from the speaker's words. Don't show tension by covering the mouth or needlessly touching the head or hair. Keep hands still unless using them in the talk.

6. **FACIAL EXPRESSIONS:** The face expresses emotion. Facial expressions help the listener understand the tone of the message. A tense speaker shows emotion on the face by grimacing or a look of fear. Be aware of what your face is doing.

7. **EYE CONTACT:** A nervous or shy person struggles with eye contact. The habit creates problems because people don't trust those who won't look them in the eye. Looking into the eyes of a listener draws them in, creating a bond. Reduce tension by making eye contact.

DRILL: Follow these drill instructions while talking into a mirror. Practice this drill once a day until you can incorporate the tips into daily conversation.

Keep these aspects in mind

Volume	Proper tone
Stand tall	Speak clearly
Use hands	Keep hands away from mouth
Facial expressions	Eye contact

TELL A MIRROR

- A funny story about yourself. Use eye contact.
- Your name, address, and telephone number.
- About a bad weather day while using facial gestures and hand movement.

- The phrase "how do you like that?" while using different voice tones (happy, sad, angry, dignified, quiet, etc.).
- The sentence: "The complex houses married and single soldiers and their families."
- A short story about a memorable moment in your life while including all eight aspects in the talk.

Reduce what is overflowing

Excitement when talking brings energy but at times overwhelms both the speaker and listener. Learn to reduce these five talking elements that unintentionally overflow due to excess nerves or excitement.

1. **TOO MUCH/LITTLE VOLUME**. The listener wants to hear the words in a comfortable volume range. Making an audience strain to hear or cover their ears from screaming prevents communication. Use voice volume like the controls on a microphone, raising or lowering the volume, depending on the audience location and size. Don't unwittingly allow a tense situation to reduce or increase volume. Keep the listener in mind. Always make sure all can hear you, the back row as well as the front row.

2. **FINGER POINTING**. Excitement causes aggression. Too much force backfires. Hand gestures add animation to conversations but can quickly turn threatening. People resent a finger in their face. Finger pointing takes on a menacing air because the speaker's overflowing emotions create unnecessary tension. The finger becomes the center of attention instead of the message. This is when two-way communication stops. Instead of pointing at someone, try pointing upward.

3. **WILDLY FLAILING ARMS**. Excited speakers flail hands and arms in unpredictably sudden directions, knocking into cups of coffee, glasses of wine, or peoples' faces. Reduce the overflowing emotion.

4. **LAUGH VOLUME AND TONE**. Everyone loves to laugh. When the laughing is loud, then go ahead and join in. But be mindful of the situation and when laughing might not be appropriate.

5. **EXCESSIVE FACIAL EXPRESSIONS**. Excitement causes excessive facial expressions. People wear emotions on their face. Be mindful of the impression your face leaves. Sour looks, disdain, menacing looks, and sad eyes affect others in many ways and most are not good. Overflowing looks create unneeded impressions.

"First master the fundamentals."

Larry Bird, NBA star

"Hidden" messages

The body communicates messages or intent in strange and mysterious ways. Sometimes unintentional physical acts seem as if the unconscious body wants to send its own hidden message through body language or voice inflection.

Let's look at a few ways the body sends "hidden" messages.

Emphasis—Be mindful of meaning

A speaker can alter the meaning of a phrase by manipulating the voice.

The most popular way involves the use of volume or tone in emphasizing certain words in a conversation.

Emphasis draws attention to the most important point in a sentence thereby directing the listener. Putting emphasis on the wrong elements, however, can bring out the worst in people and in a sentence.

Emphasis: Stress laid on a word or words to indicate special meaning or particular importance.

Clarity is difficult when speaking. The wrong emphasis on a particular word while speaking gives a less accurate meaning to a listener.

Skilled speakers influence listeners by subtly emphasizing an inflammatory or persuasive word or two in a sentence, leading listeners to where they want them to go.

The body and/or voice tone along with volume play the main roles in emphasizing a word in a sentence.

How to emphasize while talking

A speaker emphasizes by doing the following:

- Pronouncing the first syllable of a key word louder than other syllables.
- Using a lower pitch from the previous words.
- Slowly saying the key word.
- Stretching the vowel sound.
- Pausing after saying the key word.
- Using body language when saying the key word.

Emphasis brings attention to some word while reducing attention to others. The more a speaker uses these techniques, the more directly the speaker leads the listener to main points.

See how emphasizing different words in this sentence changes the meaning in this often-used example, "I didn't say she took my money." Emphasizing a different word in the sentence changes the meaning of the sentence.

- *__I__ didn't say she took my money.* Somebody else said it.
- *I __didn't__ say she took my money.* I did not say it but might have thought it or even wrote it.
- *I didn't __say__ she took my money.* I only implied it or wrote it.
- *I didn't say __she__ took my money.* I said someone did but not her.
- *I didn't say she __took__ my money.* I considered it borrowed but she didn't ask.
- *I didn't say she took __my__ money.* Only that she took someone's money.
- *I didn't say she took my __money__.* She took stuff but not money.

Speakers use emphasis to create contrast, persuasion, arousal, and distractions. Use it carefully because emphasizing a word may create a demeaning impression. Here's an example.

Snow and Sunshine are talking about Sarah.

Snow: Are you and Sarah friends?
Sunshine: I know her, but we're not friends.

Spoken without emphasis Sunshine simply says she and Sarah are not friends. Try emphasizing *but* or *not* in Sunshine's sentence to see the meaning change and not for the good.

I know her, _but_ we're not friends. (Sunshine doesn't like Sarah.)
I know her, but we're _not_ friends. (Sunshine really doesn't like Sarah.)

Let's have fun

Suggestions on ways to have fun while practicing English:

- **Speaking activity:** Say the sentence: "*John isn't going to school tomorrow*." Emphasize a different word each time. See if you can hear how the meaning of the sentence changes.

- **Shared activity:** Practice emphasizing different words in sentences in a conversation with a friend. Talk about subjects such as movies, music, or novels.

- **Let's go somewhere:** Watch a movie or television show to listen to actors use emphasis in dialogue.

"He allowed himself to be swayed by his conviction that human beings are not born once and for all on the day their mothers give birth to them, but that life obliges them over and over again to give birth to themselves."

Gabriel García Márquez, *Love in the Time of Cholera*

Body language

Many times a person says one thing while their body sends a conflicting message. The instinctual body messages often reveal the truth while the words ring false.

Here are some messages our body sends:

- **ARMS CROSSED OVER THE CHEST**. A defensive posture that says that the individual disagrees or is not open to the opinions or actions of other individuals with whom they are communicating.
- **NAIL BITING**. Nail biting shows stress, nervousness, or insecurity. Many people bite their nails without even realizing it.
- **HAND PLACED ON THE CHEEK**. This indicates a person is lost in thought, or is considering something.
- **TAPPING OR DRUMMING THE FINGERS**. Finger-tapping demonstrates a person is growing impatient or tired of waiting.
- **HEAD TILTED TO ONE SIDE**. A tilted head says a person is listening keenly, or is interested in what is being communicated.
- **TOUCHING THE NOSE**. Touching or rubbing the nose signifies a number of things. It can be a signal of disbelief or rejection, or a sign that an individual is being untruthful about what they are saying.
- **RUBBING THE HANDS TOGETHER BRISKLY**. This shows that a person's hands are cold or that an individual is excited and waiting in anticipation.
- **PLACING THE TIPS OF THE FINGERS TOGETHER**. "Steepling" of the fingers, or placing the tips of them together, is a demonstration of control and authority. This body language can be used by bosses or authority figures to subtly demonstrate that they are running things.
- **PALMS OPEN, FACING UPWARD**. A sign of openness and honesty that can be a show of submission. In older days when many people carried weapons, this was used to show that they were not holding one. Some people open their palms during worship at church as a sign of submission and respect.
- **HEAD IN HANDS**. Another example of body language that might mean a number of things. It may demonstrate boredom,

or it might show that a person is upset or ashamed and does not want to show their face.

- **LOCKED ANKLES**. Locking the ankles together while standing or seated communicates nervousness or apprehension.
- **STANDING UP STRAIGHT, SHOULDERS BACK**. This position shows a confident person and is often accompanied with walking at a brisk stride.
- **STROKING OF THE CHIN**. Stroking the chin communicates a person in deep thought. Such a motion is often used unintentionally when an individual is trying to come to a decision about a matter.
- **PULLING OF THE EAR**. People pull the lobes of one of their ears when attempting to make a decision, but remain indecisive. This motion demonstrates the inability to come to a conclusion.
- **SLUMPED SHOULDERS WITH HANDS IN POCKETS**. A "woe-is-me" pose that reflects an unconfident and insecure individual.

Body language and lies

Body language not only sends messages of indecisiveness, strength, nervousness, or impatience but also more treacherous designs such as a deceit.

Much study focuses on the ability to tell when a person tells a lie. Studies by body language professionals say that, while it may be difficult to tell when someone is lying, there are certain clues. Here are a few.

- The head moves very quickly to the side, up, or down just before responding to a question.
- The person may touch or cover their mouth, play with their hair, or fidget needlessly with their hands. Other head signs include touching the nose, scratching the ear, and rubbing the eyes.

- They will tap, shuffle, or move their feet as they talk.
- They will hide their hands under a desk or behind their back.
- They cover a vulnerable part of their body such as the throat, chest, head, or abdomen.
- Rapid blinking or no blinking at all. Some try to intimidate through staring while others continually flutter their eyes.
- They point a lot at the other person, trying to turn the tables on the accuser.

Conclusion

The body does many wonderful things for us but we too often fail to consider what the body tells others regarding our messages. We fret over mispronounced or poorly chosen words while our face looks like we just ate a lemon, our arms are tightly crossed, and our voice creaks with nervousness. The wise speaker understands the body and words work together to form a solid message.

Standing tall with a smile on our face and a strong clear voice sends a positive vibe that accentuates the spoken message.

SITUATIONS

COMMON SPEAKING CHALLENGES

Situation 1: Greetings

The most beautiful girl in the world, Paula, sat in front of me in history class. I had one big problem, I couldn't say hello. Each night I tossed and turned in bed dreaming up witty conversations with the lovely vision. But as soon as I took my seat, the words froze inside and I became a mute frog, quiet and jumpy. I just stared at her long black hair tumbling onto my desk as the well-planned words hid behind my miserable fear-laden heart. I hated seventh-grade history class.

THE MOST IMPORTANT SENTENCE in all languages is (in English):

"Hello. How are you?"

What makes the simple words critical? These tidings set into motion the potential of the evolution of a new life force by making two people into one spirit. What magical things happen by the new creation is anyone's guess.

An open, receptive greeting

Yin reflects the open and receptive element in yinyang. Letting the yin side open like a flower to new acquaintances shows accessibility as a human.

An open attitude makes a person much more potent than a judgmental one. Judging others for a different skin color, a different culture, or different clothes makes one small-minded. A wise person realizes it makes no sense to accept one person and not another.

True communication begins when the mind and heart open to new people. Getting the relationship off on the right foot takes a solid greeting.

"Only a life lived for others is a life worthwhile."

Albert Einstein

The calculating brain

Saying hello goes far beyond the word. The brain whirs into action when we meet a new person. Who that person is makes a big difference.

How do you respond when meeting this individual?

- A person the same age and sex as you
- A much older person
- A much younger person
- A person you find attractive

I'm guessing each type generates a much different result. But in each circumstance our computer-like brains calculate the answers to these questions:

- What does the person look like?
- Did they smile?
- Are their clothes neat or trendy?
- What does their hair look like?
- Did they make eye contact?
- Did they shake hands or politely nod?
- Do they seem friendly?
- What stands out?

The other person goes down the same checklist on us. The basic question each person asks is: Does this person look like they are worth my time?

Now if the person is a similar age and attractive then we may give them more of a chance. Otherwise, if the answer comes back "No" then chances are we won't even hear the greeting. But we need to fight this quick rejection.

TOP TIP
THE OTHER PERSON'S WILLINGNESS TO BE FRIENDLY IS OUT OF YOUR CONTROL.

The power of you

A friendly person does their best to put their best greeting foot forward regardless of who the other person is.

They tamp down impulses that make them too judgmental based on physical traits. They avoid thinking: "Why should I care about this stranger? What can they do for me?"

This type of thinking blocks the open and receptive yin side, making us untrustworthy. When making snap decisions about people we become unlikable and selfish.

A disingenuous person acts engaging by smiling and asking questions when they meet someone they consider worthwhile. They seek others' approval by riveting attention or over-the-top kindness. When meeting someone seen as unimportant they smile weakly, if at all, while acting disinterested or arrogant.

Don't fall into this trap. The judgmental attitude robs us of the power of our humanity. Using the powerful weapon of an open, attentive attitude makes a person a strong, kind and entertaining speaker.

Signposts to greeting magic

Greeting a person with a true kind spirit unveils a caring human being. The path to achieving this kindness requires the following steps:

1. **BE PRESENT**: The most critical element in a greeting involves being mentally present. Thinking about last night's party, hunger, or a cell phone's Twitter feed reduces the chances of making a meaningful impact. Being in the moment blocks out distractions, allowing focus on the person.

2. **BE GROUNDED**: The road to a solid greeting starts with self-knowledge. Knowing what you stand for makes meeting others easier. The other person's interests don't change your interests. Don't apologize for or hide from who you are. Can a relationship start by misleading others?

3. **RELAX**: Work to maintain a calm, relaxed mind when greeting another person. Take a deep breath, smile and start with hello. Don't overthink the situation but remain open-minded.

4. **DON'T SEEK OTHERS' APPROVAL**: Caring about others' approval makes a person a prisoner. If a person accepts who they are then another person's approval or disapproval is irrelevant. Problems only arise when trying to be something you're

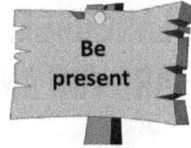

not. Eventually the truth comes out and all false efforts will have been in vain.

TOP TIP
A PERSON SAYING HELLO GETS JUDGED ON SEVERAL FACTORS INCLUDING PRONUNCIATION, VOCABULARY, CLEANLINESS, EYE CONTACT, FACIAL EXPRESSION, BODY LANGUAGE, AND DRESS. ASK YOURSELF THIS QUESTION: ARE YOU AND WHAT YOU LOOK LIKE THE SAME PERSON?

Creating one spirit

Two people become one spirit when greeting each other in a mutual bond of respect. If one person does all the talking or one person fails to actively listen or participate, then the meeting loses balance.

Both people need to be present and actively involved for a successful interaction. Keep in mind, however, that all you can do is account for yourself. If the other person fails to pay attention then feel free to disengage.

Start with an open and receptive yin side, accepting all with a non-judgmental attitude.

Keep these five points in mind when attempting to create a bond with another human being.

TOP TIP
THE POTENT COMBINATION OF KNOWING YOURSELF AND A WILLINGNESS TO GREET OTHERS WITH AN OPEN MIND CREATES A POWERFUL FORCE.

1. **BE AWARE**. An engaging attitude presents the best "you" possible. This involves actions such as speaking with polite intention, listening, and focusing on the other person.

2. **THE CONVERSATION AS ONE**. Look at a conversation as one entity, the yinyang symbol. Two become one when talking. This creates a positive atmosphere. Good conversationalists encourage conversation by discussing common topics, unifying the conversation. Research shows that imitating body gestures of conversation partners increases the likelihood of a positive reaction.

3. **CREATE BALANCE**. Create balance in conversation by asking questions. People freeze because they think "what should I talk about?" The question should be "who is the other person and what do they want to talk about?" Ask a question, step back, and listen. Let the other person talk and then provide an active and constructive response to develop balance.

"Silence is one of the great arts of conversation."

Marcus Tullius Cicero

4. **POSITIVE SPIRIT**. People prefer likeable over competent people. Create a positive spirit by giving compliments, saying positive things, and smiling. Good vibrations cement a positive encounter.

5. **CREATING LIFE**. A budding friendship comes to full bloom when two people involved in a conversation become one. The new creation with its yinyang synergy unleashes a full range of emotions, including excitement and interest. The newly-created life force grows due to the release of enthusiasm. Where it goes after its creation is anyone's guess.

The two-step hello

What's next after hello? Finding common ground is a challenge. What can you talk about with a stranger?

Follow this two-step process for meeting new people.

STEP 1: Memorize a list of general topics as conversation starters. Use the themes as a strategy to jump-start a conversation when meeting someone new.

"A man's conversation is the mirror of his thoughts."

Conversation topics for new acquaintances come from this generally accepted list of subjects. Ask questions about:

1. **FAMILY:**
   - "How many people are in your family?"
   - "Do you come from a large family?"
   - "Are you married?"
2. **FUTURE PLANS:**
   - "Do you have a busy day?"
   - "What do you do?"
   - "What are you doing for the holidays?"

3. HEALTH:
- "How are you doing today?"
- "You look very healthy."
- "Do you exercise regularly?"

4. HOBBIES:
- "Have you played this new computer game?"
- "You look like you're in good shape."
- "Do you go to a gym?"

5. MUSIC:
- "I love Taylor Swift. What about you?"
- "Do you play guitar?"

6. SCHOOL/WORK:
- "Where do you go to school?"
- "What department do you work in?"

7. SPORTS:
- "Hey, I see you are wearing a Kobe Bryant shirt. Do you like basketball?"
- "Do you like to jog?"

8. RECENT PAST:
- "Did you just move here?"
- "What's your home town?"

9. PETS:
- "Do you have a pet?"
- "What's its name?"

10. MUTUAL FRIENDS:
- "How did you meet ___?"
- "How long have you known ___?"
- "____ likes gardening. Do you garden too?"

STEP 2: This step requires considering which of the 10 topic areas create the best-suited conversation. Where does the common ground lie between you and this person?

Talking to someone who just moved to town about their new home makes good sense. Talking to them about local issues that they wouldn't be aware of or personal issues like how much money they make or health issues does not make sense.

Once the conversation starts, then let it go wherever by following up with questions. If the topic dies out, then transition to another one.

Act like a miner looking for gold. If you find the right spot then start digging for a new friend.

Question of the day

Talk about the following question with a friend or form an opinion on your own. Read the conversation between Emmett, Edie and Iris and then consider how you would respond. Discuss your answer with a friend. Remember to say why you think or feel as you do.

Question: What do you say when you first meet someone?

- **Iris:** I find it difficult to speak to someone for the first time. I am a little shy and have no idea what the person likes to do. I usually just ask them their name and where they're from. Then it usually turns awkwardly silent.
- **Emmett:** I talk about a lot of things when meeting a new person. I ask questions like "What music do you like?" "Do you play sports?" "Where do you live?" or "What games do you play on your phone?" It's easy if you smile and act interested.

- **Edie:** I have no interest in meeting new people. If a friend introduces me to someone then I keep my headphones on or pretend to be checking my phone. It's a hassle meeting new people. They cause trouble or want to do things I have no interest in.

What do you say or do when meeting a new person? Do you find it easy, difficult or not worth the time?

Let's have fun

Suggestions on ways to have fun while practicing English:

- **Speaking activity:** The next time meeting someone, ask a question or two about who they are and what they like to do. Play detective by using visual clues they provide with the way they dress and look. Then ask appropriate questions.

- **Shared activity:** Have fun with a friend by asking outlandish questions that you wouldn't normally ask a new acquaintance. (Examples: "Have you ever met an alien?" "Do you believe in reincarnation?" or "How high is up?")

- **Let's go somewhere:** Go to a farmers' market to buy some fruits and vegetables. Introduce yourself to the farmers then ask questions about growing crops and producing products.

Good or bad impression?

Meeting a new person creates a first impression. First meetings establish a wide range of emotions from "WOW! I love that guy" to "Oh, what a slob."

FIRST IMPRESSION: The initial impression we have of another person when we meet them for the first time. It includes positive and negative impressions and a sense of physical and psychological features.

The cliché "No one ever gets a second chance at making a first impression" is true. Some go well while other first impressions go sideways when interests substantially vary. They may love Italian shoes and your basketball sneakers leave them cold. Oh well!

People have personal interests, tastes, prejudices, dressing styles, and emotions. Styles may mesh or clash. Don't take it personally.

But when meeting a person don't assume you know who they are by how they look. The clues they give may be misleading. Don't attempt to guess what the new person likes or dislikes. Just ask.

An open-minded person does their best not to prejudge. If a person prejudges you, then so be it. Not everyone becomes a friend, and that's OK. Don't stop trying because a few people don't get it.

TOP TIP
A GENUINE PERSON KNOWS AND ACCEPTS WHO THEY ARE.

Visual clues

A first impression is like a mystery game where the detective searches for clues regarding a suspect. Read the clues, come up with questions, and see where they take you. Be careful of misleading clues!

- What clothes are they wearing? A sports shirt? Designer clothes?
- What are they carrying? A book bag? A tennis racquet? A cup of coffee?
- Where did you meet them? At the gym? At school? At a restaurant?
- Do they have a tattoo, earrings, or blue hair?

Small details reveal a glimpse of the individual. Add up the clues and a picture of the person begins to emerge. The details provide fodder for questions to ask to determine the accuracy of the clues. But be careful because people are sensitive.

My son, who is tall, didn't like it when people always assumed he played basketball. He would curtly respond to the question, "Do you play basketball?" by replying "No. Do you play miniature golf?"

People tire of obvious questions so try to be creative when asking about a standout feature like height, hair, or weight.

Again, don't prejudge. Ask questions. Wrongly presuming a person's culture, knowledge, or beliefs can create unnecessary tension.

"Let us always meet each other with a smile for the smile is the beginning of love."

Mother Teresa

Fly your own flag

Make a great first impression by simply being genuine. A sincere person gracefully accepts who they are.

Don't hide your true self by being disingenuous. Great people come in all shapes, sizes and colors! Accept your shyness, nerdy intellectualism, purple hair, or foreign culture. Let your flag fly. You'll impress people by being who you are.

But don't feel the need to shove your uniqueness down the throat of a new acquaintance. Trying too hard to be genuine achieves the opposite effect.

People who try too hard to look young—like the 50-year-old going for the 20-something look—appear old. The overbearing individual attempting to be too kind becomes unbearable.

Pushing too hard to show your true self lacks stability, leading to bad impressions. You'll impress by not trying to impress.

Make a good impression by "being there"

A professional sports adage says: "The most important ability is availability." If you're not playing due to injury then all your talent does the team no good.

This applies to meeting a new person as well. If you take the time to meet a new person then "be there" for them. A few tips:

1. **SMILE POLITELY.** Make strong eye contact and say hello.
2. **SHAKE HANDS.** Do this if appropriate but remember some cultures do not shake hands, so a quick decision must be made.
3. **USE OPEN, FRIENDLY BODY LANGUAGE.** Arms down, posture tall with shoulders slightly back, and head upright sends an open for business message.

4. **ASK.** Incorporate appropriate questions.
5. **SHOW A KEEN INTEREST.** Avoid making too many self-centered comments unless asked. Direct conversation to the other person.
6. **AVOID.** Don't discuss health issues, age, financial status, political views, controversial topics, and gossip.
7. **END THE CONVERSATION.** Finish by saying how you enjoyed meeting and exchange contact information if appropriate. **Important**: End the conversation by saying the person's name such as "John, it was nice to meet you." People love to hear their name!

Unimpressive showing

People give bad first impressions without ever knowing it. People can easily spot a poor visual cue that says "I don't want to talk to you."

The yinyang of first impressions

1. Smile
2. Shake hands
3. Open body language
4. Ask questions
5. Show interest
6. Avoid controversy
7. End politely

1. Yawning
2. Fold arms across chest
3. Use cellphone
4. No eye contact
5. Make faces
6. Look around

Keep these suggestions in mind to avoid an unimpressive first meeting:

1. **YAWNING**: Nothing says "you are boring" more than a big yawn.
2. **ARMS FOLDED ACROSS THE CHEST**: Holding arms tight across the chest signals "I'm not interested in you."
3. **PLAYING WITH A CELL PHONE**: If the phone is more interesting than the person then what's the point? Playing with a phone shows a lack of character. Leave the phone in the pocket or purse. It's not that important and shows insecurity.
4. **AVOIDING EYE CONTACT**: Look people in the eyes when meeting them. No eye contact says a person is shy, distrustful, or disinterested.
5. **MAKING FACES**: An unwelcoming look on the face, rolling the eyes, or a bored look make others uncomfortable. Always ask "What's my face saying?"
6. **LOOKING AROUND**. Glancing past the person or turning around says "I have no interest in you or what you're saying. I'm looking for someone more important."

A good first impression often means just not making a bad first impression.

Let's have fun

Suggestions on ways to have fun while practicing English:

- **Speaking activity:** Come up with unique questions in each of the 10 topic areas such as "Have you ever had a pet snake?" Off-the-wall questions are great attention-getters.

- **Shared activity:** Practice asking unique questions from each topic area on friends over the next week. Notice your friends' reactions. See if you can carry on a discussion for at least one minute for each question.

- **Let's go somewhere:** Prepare unique questions to ask at the next party you attend. Don't be shy. Chances are the questions become the hit of the party.

Conversation: Greeting and introduction

Here is a conversation involving four people, Snow, Sunshine, Sam, and Spike. See how each person uses the others' names in the conversation. This engages people in the conversation and helps each person remember the others' names. Emphasize underlined and italicized words.

Snow and Sunshine are shopping at the mall for summer clothes. Snow sees her friend, Sam, and introduces him to Sunshine. Sam is with another boy who Snow does not know.

Snow: *(Waves to Sam.)* Sam. Good to see you! How are *you*? I can't believe *you're* shopping.

Sam: *(Walks up to Snow and smiles at her.)* Nice to see you, Snow. *(He shakes her hand.)* No shopping for me! I am here with my friend, *Spike*. We are going to the movies in 20 minutes.

Snow: Hello *Spike*. Let me introduce you to my friend, *Sunshine*. She *lives* on the other side of town but we used to be neighbors. Sam and Spike, this is *Sunshine*.

Sam: Hello Sunshine. Nice to _meet_ you. *(He looks her in the eyes and nods politely.)*

Spike: Hey _Sunshine_. *(He looks her in the eyes and nods politely.)*

Sunshine: Nice to meet you guys. Snow told me about _you,_ Sam. *(She nods and smiles at Sam while saying "you.")*

Sam: Oh, what did _she_ (nodding at Snow) say? I hope it was _good_.

Snow: _Of course_ it was good, Sam! Hey, I have to use the restroom. You three talk and I'll be _back_ in a minute.

Sam: Sure. So, Sunshine, what are _you_ shopping for today?

Sunshine: _Summer_ clothes. Snow and I are going on vacation with my parents _next week_.

Sam: That sounds _fun_. Where are you _going_?

Sunshine: To the ocean. Are _you_ going on vacation this summer?

Sam: No. Spike and I are going to _summer school_.

Sunshine: Do you _need_ to go?

Spike: No. I just want to take a course on _rockets_.

Sunshine: Wow. You must be _smart_.

Snow: I'm back.

Sam: Well we have to go. Good meeting you, Sunshine. Let's get together after your vacation. You can tell me _all_ about it.

Snow: Sure. See you, Sam. You _too_, Spike.

Sam: Bye, you two.

Let's have fun

Suggestions on ways to have fun while practicing English:

- **Speaking activity:** Think about people you see on a regular basis but don't know. Say hello next time you see them.

- **Shared activity:** The next time out with a friend or relative play a game. Take turns saying hello to people you don't know but who appear to be friendly. The person who gets the most hellos back is the winner. Just remember to be polite.

- **Let's go somewhere:** Go to a local festival, school activity, playground, or location with familiar faces. Have fun introducing yourselves to other people.

Conclusion

Saying hello to a new person can seem threatening. Speaking to Paula in seventh grade scared me to the point of not being able to sleep. The fear is real.

Indeed, the path to light seems very dark. How can you make progress in life if you can't say hello?

If fear prevents you from saying hello, then consider starting with one of these baby steps. A small bit of positive feedback may be all it takes to plant the seeds of friendship.

- **START WITH A SMILE.** Smiling creates a sense of openness. If a person responds with a smile, then take the next step.
- **BE OPEN.** Practice by nodding your head and smiling at others

when walking down the street or shopping. Not everyone will respond, but many will. A smile, along with open and active eyes, reveals a friendly person.

- **PREPARE**. If there is someone you want to meet, then do a little research and discover something about them, such as what they enjoy doing. A little preparation shows interest. Just don't go overboard since too much research may scare them away.
- **ASK A QUESTION**. If you see someone on a regular basis that you want to meet, then think of a question to ask. The question can be as simple as, "How are you doing today?"

Fear creates a great illusion. Conquer fear, say hello and realize how many things open up.

Situation 2: Making friends

The coach put me in left field to start the baseball game. I wanted to make a good impression because I didn't know anyone on the team. The first batter hit a line drive right at me. I misjudged the ball and it flew over my head for an error. My mistake cost the team several runs. When the inning ended, I sat at the end of the bench feeling embarrassed. A teammate sat next to me smiling and said, "Hey, I'm Rick. Don't worry about it. We're here to have fun." Laughing together, we soon became best friends.

The saying goes "to have a friend, be a friend." Warm and understanding friendship makes life worth living. Companionship reveals a yinyang relationship, allowing friends to grow separately without growing apart.

This chapter focuses on finding a friend and being a friend. Speaking plays a crucial role in this process because words guide and encourage relationships.

The give and take of friendship

Why do some people find it easy to make new friends while others struggle? People who excel at friendship understand the give-and-take process of making a friend.

TOP TIP

MOST PEOPLE WANT MORE FRIENDS. DON'T BE EMBARRASSED ABOUT TRYING TO MAKE NEW FRIENDS. SOMEONE NEEDS TO MAKE THE FIRST MOVE. WHY SHOULDN'T IT BE YOU?

The signposts along the path to making a friend

1. **IT'S NOT ALL ABOUT YOU:** Everybody wins when it comes to friendship. Both sides need to feel positive about the relationship. Self-centered individuals who want all the attention may find difficulty in developing friends. If struggling to make friends then step back and understand that friends do not exist solely as your audience. Great friends understand give and take.

2. **SET THE RIGHT TONE:** A person who makes friends easily sets the right tone. This includes

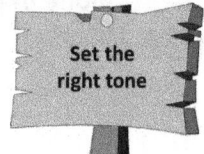

Set the right tone

smiling, listening, and asking questions. These engaging characteristics make a speaker enjoyable.

3. **A NEW WAY TO LIVE**: New friends bring ideas and experiences into another's life. This requires not being a slave to a past agenda but being open to new ideas. An "I always do it this way" mentality chases people away. New friends bring new energy and you need to embrace it.

Be open to new ways

4. **TOO MUCH FORCE BACKFIRES**: Pushing too hard stops many friendships before they take root. Excessive excitement may chase away a new friend. A friendship grows like a rose, at its own pace. Too much water or sunlight kills a budding rose before it ever blooms. Give a new friendship time to strengthen.

Easy does it

A friend's words...

A friend's words provide...

1. **HONESTY**. Friends rely on one another for true words.
2. **RESPECT**. A companion values what you say.

"I would rather walk with a friend in the dark than walk alone in the light."

Helen Keller

3. **SUPPORT**. A friend's word provides encouragement.
4. **GOOD LISTENING SKILLS**. A friend hears and responds to what you say.
5. **FUN**. A pal brings enjoyable conversation.

Let's have fun

Suggestions on ways to have fun while practicing English:

- **Activity:** Are you a good friend? Look at the five qualities a friend's conversation brings to the relationship. Which ones describe you and which ones cause trouble? Make two columns, listing your strengths and weaknesses.

- **Shared Activity:** Talk with a friend and discuss the qualities of friendship. Ask if you need to improve any basic friendship qualities. Tell your friend your thoughts of them only if asked. Agree not to be sensitive with the outcome!

Question of the day

Talk about the following question with a friend or consider your own view. Read the conversation between Emmett, Iris and Edie. Then discuss the question with a friend and share your answers. Remember to explain why you think and feel as you do.

**Question: What's the difference between
a good friend and a bad friend?**

- **Iris**: I don't think there are bad friends. Sometimes friends do bad things but that doesn't make them bad friends. I think when a friend does something wrong then a true friend tries to help.
- **Emmett**: Sometimes that's not always true. People change. I had a good friend when I was young but as we got older, we started doing different things. He got into trouble by hanging out with a rough crowd. We became different people and drifted apart. I am glad we did!
- **Edie**: Friends come and go like the leaves on a tree. Do the best you can with them while they're here and remember them fondly when they're gone.

What do you think?

Let's have fun

Suggestions on ways to have fun while practicing English:

- **Shared activity:** Ask people their opinion on "bad" friends. Have they ever had one? If they did, then ask them to talk about the circumstances.

Buried treasures

Finding a friend can be like coming across a hidden fortune. The effort may be challenging but an open and determined effort often leads to new acquaintances much like discovering and cherishing a buried treasure.

Places to find new friends

Most good friends enjoy doing similar things. That's what makes them so fun. Where can you find them? Here are a few suggestions:

1. **JOIN AN ORGANIZATION OR CLUB**: Age-appropriate groups of people who share common interests are a good place to start. A group exists for every conceivable interest. The Internet provides information on where to find them.

TOP TIP
A GOOD FRIEND IS LIKE A FOUR-LEAF CLOVER; HARD TO FIND AND LUCKY TO HAVE!

2. **SIGN UP FOR A SPORTS TEAM OR CLUB SPORT**: Sports teams and clubs offer a wide range of physical activities. Either team sports like baseball, basketball, kickball, and soccer or club or individual sports such as running, ping-pong, or golf are available in every city and town.

3. **VOLUNTEER**: Great people make great communities. Volunteering makes neighborhoods better while providing a place to meet others who think like you. Nursing homes, food banks, hospitals, environmental groups, and non-profit organizations need people to assist in a wide range of activities.

4. **SOMEONE NEW**: People move from one city to another all the time. Welcome new people by showing them around town. It's the neighborly thing to do.

5. **MAKE SOMETHING HAPPEN**: Don't sit waiting for new friends to knock on the door. Get out and create reasons for people to get together. Organize an effort to clean up a park, start a walking club, or invite classmates or fellow employees to get together. Be the straw that stirs the drink!

6. **SIT SOMEWHERE NEW**: Change seats to change life. Sit with someone new on the bus, at lunch, in class, at work, or anywhere you sit. Get out of the same old seat and alter life by moving around.

Let's have fun

Suggestions on ways to have fun while practicing English:

- **Studying activity:** Make a list of five things to do to make new friends. Pick one of the five and try it.

- **Shared activity:** Talk to friends or relatives and ask them where they have found friends during their lifetime.

- **Let's go somewhere:** Come up with an idea to bring people together to improve the community, office, neighborhood, or school. This includes cleaning up an area, holding a joint yard sale, or having a group picnic. Share ideas with a neighbor, friend, or classmate. Sometimes these ideas take time to take hold. Don't give up easily.

Nice people have more friends

Why do some people have lots of friends? They attract new people to them like fleas to a dog.

Do they enjoy a mysterious magnetic quality that fascinates people? Well, maybe a few do, but most friendly people possess certain qualities that shout "Hey, I like you."

What are those qualities? Not necessarily beauty or brains. A research study by the University of California at Los Angeles found that people like sincere and understanding people not necessarily beautiful or smart ones.

"Fortune favors the prepared mind."

Louis Pasteur

How to be "likeable"

How do you get people to "like" you? Sure, you can buy gifts or give never-ending compliments. But truly likeable people share these common traits.

1. **GOOD ATTITUDE**. People like enthusiastic and positive people. Bad attitudes attract nothing but trouble.
2. **ASK QUESTIONS**. Flatter people by asking them questions. It shows interest.
3. **PUTS AWAY THE PHONE**. Don't let people think the phone is more important to you than they are.
4. **IS GENUINE**. Nobody likes a fake. Often goofy or off-the-wall qualities serve as an individual's best qualities so don't hide them.
5. **DOESN'T PASS JUDGMENT**. Judging others makes you appear mean-spirited.
6. **DOESN'T SEEK ATTENTION**. Attentive and friendly gets more positive attention than saying "look at me." Thank others for help when you are the center of attention. Stay humble.

7. **USES POSITIVE BODY LANGUAGE**. Use inviting body language such as leaning slightly in when listening to others, uncrossing your arms, maintaining a positive tone of voice, and keeping good eye contact.

8. **SMILES**. Nice people smile. A lot.

9. **MAKES A STRONG FIRST IMPRESSION**. The first meeting often determines if people become friends so be on your toes and do your best by smiling, asking questions, and listening.

10. **GREETS PEOPLE BY NAME**. Remember people's names and use them. Greeting people by name wins friends.

11. **PUTS IT ALL TOGETHER**. Likeable people bring out the best in everyone. Keep these traits in mind to be the person everyone wants to know.

Let's have fun

Suggestions on ways to have fun while practicing English:

- **Studying activity:** Think about a friendly person. Write down the reasons why people like this person.

- **Shared activity:** Practice two or three of the 11 likeability tips for one week. See if one of the tips affects your conversations more than the others. Change tips after one week. Determine the easiest and most effective tips.

- **Let's go somewhere:** Make a date to see a person everyone likes, such as the city's mayor, a successful businessperson, or a popular teacher. Ask why they think people like them.

Active listening

A section on the importance of active listening needs to be in every chapter of this book. This essential element needs to be a part of your life whether you're making a friend, running a company, or talking to your mother.

Active listening: A communication technique used in counseling, training, and conflict resolution requiring the listener to fully concentrate, understand, respond, and then remember what is being said.

Harvard University did a study on active listening and concluded that people spent half of work time listening, but immediately forgot half of the things heard.

Do you instantly forget half of what friends say? Maybe you're not the friend you think you are.

Active listening improves friendship

If you want to be liked then start listening. The Harvard study said that active listening accounts for 40% of likeability as a person. Here's how listening builds friendship:

1. **INCREASES TRUST.** Listening and asking questions shows interest which leads to trust.
2. **DIMINISHES CONFLICTS.** Active listening—immediately asking questions and clarifying misunderstandings—reduces the chances for disagreements between people.
3. **PROVIDES MOTIVATION.** Asking questions and giving encouragement brings energy that motivates others.

4. **INSPIRES CONFIDENCE**. Active listening allows others to work through situations through questioning. This process builds confidence.

Active listening does not mean just zipping the mouth shut. It's a skill that involves understanding friends and business associates, getting them to talk more, and inspiring trust and commitment.

TOP TIP
RESEARCH SAYS POOR LISTENING DIMINISHES THE ABILITY TO CREATE A POSITIVE CONNECTION WITH OTHERS, NEGATIVELY IMPACTING LEADERSHIP ABILITY.

The "hidden secrets" to making friends

Up until this point, we've given well-established ideas on making friends. Now we'll reveal the **hidden secrets** to developing lifelong friendships.

These mysterious ways establish bonds that run deep into the spirit of humans. They develop roots so that relationships remain firmly grounded in respect and understanding.

Use these techniques wisely.

1. **COMPETE WITH NO ONE SO NO ONE CAN COMPETE WITH YOU.** Competition ruins many friendships. Trying to be better than others leads to poor decisions and bad choices of words. Avoid competing with friends. Pursue excellence not success.
2. **COMPETE WITH A SENSE OF PLAY**. While encouraging a noncompetitive attitude, friends engage in competitive activities

like ping-pong and cards. Play to win, but remember to compete with a sense of play. Don't get serious by turning a positive, fun-loving situation into a death match. Congratulate winners and losers while graciously accepting winning and losing.

3. **LEARN HOW MUCH LITTLE WILL DO**. Life takes small amounts of effort to create giant amounts of positive influence. Saying kind words to struggling people, helping without being asked, and understanding without being told create deep impressions. Remember to be grateful to friends.

4. **TRYING TO MAKE PEOPLE HAPPY LAYS THE GROUND-WORK FOR MISERY**. Always working to make others happy creates pressure on the relationship and results in inevitable misery. Just be yourself not a happy machine. Happiness may be a byproduct of friendship from time to time, but when it's not, that's OK too.

5. **LEARN TO SEE THINGS BACKWARD, UPSIDE-DOWN, AND INSIDE-OUT**. An excellent friend sees all angles of a relationship whether backward, inside-out or upside-down. See, listen, understand, and empathize when unusual situations arise.

6. **BE ALWAYS AT EASE, OVERCOME WITHOUT COMPETING; ARRIVE WITHOUT BEING SUMMONED.** Friends don't cause tension. Be calm when dealing with friends. Don't compete and help without being asked. Doing this creates a truly valued friend.

Massive friend growth

Making a new friend creates a life force. This force has massive ability to grow exponentially and change the world.

Exponential growth: Growth whose rate becomes ever more rapid in proportion to the growing total number or size.

The life force multiplies at a staggering rate when friends introduce new friends to their friends. Look how quickly friends can grow:

- Two people meet and create a friendship
- They both introduce each other to a friend so now there are four friends
- Four friends do the same and now we have eight friends
- Repeating this three more times and you'd have 64 friends from the seeds of one friendship!

I have been a part of this magical friendship growth several times in my life. I joined a social club several years ago and within two years I had made over 400 acquaintances from the power of exponential friendship. The ability to "grow" friends at an amazing pace is true power.

Growing friendships generate amazing goodwill. I introduced two people at a Valentine's Day party several years ago. Today they remain an inseparable couple, deeply in love. They lavish unnecessary praise on me each time we meet. The simple act of introducing two people can create love in the world, the greatest act of a human being.

Keys to introducing people

When introducing two people to one another:

1. Introduce the higher ranking, older guest, customer, teacher, or senior person first. Then introduce the lower ranking, younger, host, employee, student, or junior person.
2. Tell each person the other person's name or let them tell each other their names.
3. Tell them how you know each of them and a bit of information about each person.
4. Tell them why you think they should know each other.
5. Let them talk together without interrupting unless asked a question. If they remain silent then ask one of them a question.

Let's have fun

Suggestions on ways to have fun while practicing English:

- **Speaking activity:** Think about two friends who do not know each other but who could become friends. Bring them together and see what happens.

- **Shared activity:** Ask someone you respect such as an older friend, employer or relative to introduce you to a friend or business acquaintance. Prepare questions and see what you learn from the interaction.

- **Let's go somewhere:** Go to a place where either you or a friend may see people you know such as a school sporting event, a local festival, or local restaurant. Introduce each other to anyone that one of you knows.

Conversation: Making a friend

In this conversation, Sam and Snow meet someone new named Spike. They see their friend Sunshine at a party and introduce her to Spike. Notice how Spike starts the conversation by saying he recognizes Sunshine. Remember to emphasize the underlined words.

Sam: Hello Spike. How <u>are</u> you?

Spike: I'm great. Who's <u>your</u> friend?

Sam: Oh. This is <u>Snow</u>. She is my classmate.

Snow: Hello. Did you say your name is Spike? That's an <u>interesting</u> name.

Spike: Yeah. It is a <u>nickname</u>. My name is Thomas, but my dad started calling me Spike when I was a <u>baby</u>. Hey, do you know that girl over there? She looks <u>familiar</u>.

Snow: Yes. That's <u>Sunshine</u>. Hey, Sunshine, come over here.

Sunshine: Hey, Snow. What's <u>up</u>? Long time no <u>see</u>. Hey, Sam.

Snow: Sunshine, this is <u>Spike</u>. He says you look familiar.

Sam: He says that to <u>everyone</u> he wants to meet. (Sam smiles at Spike.)

Spike: No, I have seen <u>you</u> around campus. Do you eat lunch in Canteen 1?

Sunshine: Sometimes. I <u>usually</u> have lunch there on Monday, Wednesday, and Friday. The other days, I do <u>volunteer</u> work.

Spike: What kind of volunteering do you <u>do</u>?

Sunshine: I <u>teach</u> young children English. It's fun!

Sam: How did you <u>start</u> doing that?

Sunshine: My mom's <u>friend</u> teaches at the school and got me started.

Snow: Do they need <u>more</u> help? <u>I</u> want to become a teacher.

Sunshine: I'm not sure. <u>Let</u> me find out for you.

Let's have fun

Suggestions on ways to have fun while practicing English:

- **Shared activity:** Create regular reasons to get together with friends. Good ideas include a book club, a walking or running club, regular lunches or dinners, or movie night. Encourage people to bring others to the activity so that more friends might be found.

Conclusion: A final word on friends

Making friends creates excitement in life and reveals new things. Fresh relationships open up the mind to unfamiliar yet exciting concepts, introduces different people, and increases life's fun quotient.

But keep in mind these sobering thoughts regarding friends.

1. **NOTHING IS PERMANENT**. Friends come and go. Enjoy them but realize life moves on and friends might too, for both good and bad reasons. Learn from them while embracing the wonderful opportunity to enjoy today. Be present with friends for they will eventually go.
2. **CONTROL YOUR WORLD**. Meeting new people introduces fresh things and situations. But YOU remain in control of your

life. Not all people who appear to be friends are friends. A person with strong character does what's right regardless of circumstances or what "friends" suggest. Walk away from people if you feel uncomfortable about what they do or ask of you.

3. **FRESH AIR**. A breath of fresh air comes into life when meeting a new friend. Relax and enjoy the friendship. Breathe deeply and enjoy the invigorating spirit.

4. **START SLOW**. Don't overthink or overwhelm new friends. People chase away new acquaintances by being too friendly. Start friendships by showing strength and confidence. Slowly let it blossom like a flower. Asking new friends to do something every day can make them feel uncomfortable.

5. **STAY POSITIVE**. Being a positive friend ripples out to the neighborhood which impacts the community that improves the state or province which helps the nation and eventually the world, making this a better universe. It all starts with you.

Situation 3: Compliments

Ten sleepy students made it to Monday morning English literature class. The friendly middle-aged college professor came in a few minutes late. She wore large attractive sunglasses. Trying to give her a funny compliment, I said, "Hey, nice sunglasses. Did you stay up too late last night?" I laughed. She took her sunglasses off, revealing bloodshot, tear-stained eyes. "My best friend died yesterday, and I cried all night." I wanted to disappear underneath my desk. I learned mixing compliments and humor is like mixing water and hot grease, a surefire way to have something blow up in your face.

People love compliments. Ears perk up, smiles spread across faces, and complexions blush. But giving a compliment requires a delicate touch.

"Everyone loves a compliment."

Abraham Lincoln

Keys to compliments

Whom to compliment

Whom people compliment reveals more about them than it does the receiver. Compliments ring hollow if given only to those who sit in a position to give benefits.

Compliment: A remark that expresses praise or admiration of someone.

Complimenting an attractive girl, a boss, or a teacher is like trying to sweet talk a policeman out of a ticket. You're not the first and you won't be the last.

Pretty or powerful people hear compliments as often as teachers hear excuses. Obvious attempts to curry favor by using sweet words usually fall on deaf ears. Kind, dedicated, and thoughtful people make the world a better place to live. They deserve our encouragement and compliments.

Here's our list of people or actions that should receive praise:

1. **KIND PEOPLE**: Thoughtful, compassionate people need encouragement.

   Kind people

2. **THE STRUGGLING**: All face hard times in life. When a struggling person tries to recover from a tough blow, a nice word serves as inspiration. Don't criticize or feel sorry for those grappling with life, but give hope through encouraging words.

   The struggling

3. **ACTIONS**: Compliment positive action. Physically attractive people receive many compliments for their looks. They expect them. Complimenting their positive actions carries greater weight.

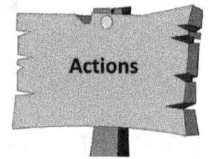

   Actions

4. **EFFORT**: Those putting out great effort deserve encouraging words. This type of praise holds tremendous influence, especially for the young. Noticing effort often creates greater effort.

5. **ANYONE WHO DESERVES ONE**: Don't only compliment friends and family. Anyone who does a kind, thoughtful act or makes an effort worth noting deserves kind words, including enemies and rivals. Nothing disarms an opponent like kind words. Spreading positive feelings to the unknown ripples out much farther than you realize. People remember your kind words long after you've forgotten them.

   Anybody who deserves one

TOP TIP
EXCESSIVE COMPLIMENTS TO THOSE WITH SOMETHING TO GIVE OFTEN LEADS TO THE OPPOSITE RESULT.

What makes a good compliment?

Effective compliments dwell in reality. Trying to create or inflate others' illusions of themselves through false praise does a disservice to all involved.

Inflating another's ego with false claims requires a continual stream of worthless words. Additionally, reputations suffer from poor judgment or deceitful motives.

When complimenting another:

1. **SOUND SINCERE**. A compliment said as a joke will be taken as a joke or an insult, not as flattering words.
2. **STICK TO FACTS**. Base compliments in fact. False compliments offend people or wrongly flatter them. Saying someone looks good when they feel fat only highlights the problem to them. Be precise in the choice of words.
3. **BACK IT UP**. Prepare to back up compliments with facts. An example: "You look nice today. Those colors look good on you." Remember the why.
4. **SMILE BUT DON'T LAUGH**. Laughing while complimenting makes the compliment appear insincere. Smile but don't laugh.
5. **COMPLIMENT ACTION**. Compliment what people do. A person enjoys "Nice job on the speech" more than "That's a nice dress."
6. **AVOID BACKHANDED COMPLIMENTS**. A backhanded compliment disguises insult. Saying "You're a good baseball player for a girl" or "Those pants make you look skinny" come off as insults. The person hears "You still aren't a good baseball player" or "You look overweight every other day."
7. **COMPLIMENT OPPONENTS**: A true champion values their opponent. They see the true yinyang dynamic in play when two

people seek a common goal. You are one. Praise the efforts of opponents instead of making them evil.

Let's have fun

Suggestions on ways to have fun while practicing English:

- List five people who deserve compliments for effort or actions. Compliment them when you see them. Determine whether the compliment comes out well or awkward. Improve delivery as needed.

Question of the day

Talk about the following question with a friend or form an opinion on your own. Read the conversation between Emmett, Iris and Edie and then consider how you would respond. Remember to explain your reasoning.

Question: Do you need to know a person to give them a compliment?

- **Emmett:** I think you need to know a person to compliment them. I could never walk up to a stranger and say something personal to them. I think it would sound insincere.
- **Iris:** Oh, Emmett, you are so shy. If I see a stranger on the bus with a beautiful smile, I always say "You have such a friendly smile." Why shouldn't we give deserving compliments to whomever? Plus, it shows you're not saying nice things just to get something in return.
- **Edie:** I don't compliment friends or strangers. I think most people

who give them are self-serving and want to get something off unsuspecting, gullible people. If someone does a nice thing then a sincere "thanks" works best for me.

What do you think? Do you compliment strangers or find it uncomfortable or impolite?

Examples of compliments

Emphasizing key words in a compliment makes the compliment zing. A few examples of compliments using emphasis:

- "Hey, Mom, dinner was _great_ tonight. I _really_ like your green beans."
- "Sue, you're a _whiz_ in math class. You knew _all_ the answers to the quiz."
- "Tom you're getting _much_ better at playing the guitar. You must be practicing _a lot_."
- "_Thanks,_ Grandma, for taking me to the store. I _enjoy_ the time we spend together."

Compliment places

Do you have trouble giving compliments? Think where instead of who. Certain locations almost require giving compliments. Keep these places in mind when visiting others.

Practice saying each compliment, emphasizing one of the words in the sentence. Try emphasizing another word to see if it sounds better.

1. **VISITING SOMEONE'S HOME**. People enjoy hearing good things about where they live.
   - "You have a great house."
   - "I love your bedroom posters."
   - "Grandma, I love your new couch."
   - "This television is awesome."
2. **EATING WITH OTHER PEOPLE**. Sitting and enjoying food together provides opportunities for a compliment.
   - "This is a wonderful restaurant you picked out."
   - "Mom, you make the best spaghetti in the world."
   - "It was very nice of you to invite me to sit with you at lunch. Thanks."
3. **DURING AN ACTIVITY**. Sports, music, or arts and crafts provide many chances to say nice things about others.
   - "Great play, Ann."
   - "You have a lovely singing voice."
   - "Wow! Your painting has really improved."
4. **AT SCHOOL OR WORK**. School and work provide opportunities to give others encouragement.
   - "Can you help me with this math question? You are so good at it."
   - "You look really pretty in that outfit, Nancy."
   - "Thanks, Mr. Smith, for taking time to help me with this question."

Giving compliments becomes habit forming. Once you start, the more you give them. Thinking beyond superficial qualities and acquaintances to action, place and strangers expands the number of opportunities to give compliments.

Let's have fun

Suggestions on ways to have fun while practicing English:

- **Speaking activity:** Come up with two unique places where compliments can be given. An example may be the grocery store. Practice giving a compliment in unique locations.
- **Shared activity:** Talk to others about when or if they give compliments. Is it easy or hard for them to praise others? Find out why.
- **Let's go somewhere:** Go for a walk and find three people to give random compliments to along the way.

Conversation: Giving a compliment

Notice Spike's honesty when giving a compliment to Sam's mother about her spaghetti. Spike really likes the food and wants to tell Sam's mother that he does. Practice the use of emphasis.

Sam's mother, Mrs. Jones, asks Spike to have dinner with their family after he gives Sam soccer tips at the park. Spike's mother says it is OK, and Sam and Spike show up hungry.

Mrs. Jones: Please sit _here_, Spike, next to Sam.

Spike: Thank you Mrs. Jones. I _sure_ am hungry.

Sam: We are having spaghetti, Spike. Do _you_ like it?

Spike: Great. I _love_ it. My mother is Italian and makes spaghetti _every_ Sunday. I especially love _meatballs_.

Mrs. Jones: (Giving Spike a large plate of spaghetti and two meatballs) _Here_ you go, Spike.

Spike: This _smells_ as good as my mom's spaghetti, Mrs. Jones. You must be an Italian _chef_! I usually _never_ like any spaghetti but Mom's.

Mrs. Jones: Thank you, Spike. I'm not Italian or a chef but I _do_ like to cook for hungry boys. With compliments like that, you can come for dinner _anytime_.

Compliment considerations

Troubles arise from giving, receiving and misusing compliments. The issue usually involves the emotion of insecurity.

Let's look at the difference between a confident person and an insecure one when giving compliments.

Saying nice words

A compliment simply points out an individual's good qualities. That why people love them.

Confident people give compliments because they understand the power in shifting the focus of attention to others in the conversation. Complimenting others as more capable or superior to oneself signals strength and character. True leaders practice this trait.

Also a confident individual doesn't fear that giving positive attention to others will be rejected or seen as too forward. A compliment reflects a simple statement of fact.

When giving a compliment…

1. **DON'T WORRY**. Always remember EVERYONE loves to hear nice things about themselves.
2. **PREPARE**. Think carefully. Prepare words in an easy-to-understand but precise way to make the compliment honest.

3. **SAY IT IN PRIVATE**. Give a compliment in private to a shy person. A public compliment may embarrass the receiving person. Also, a kind word in private appears less self-serving.

4. **DON'T EXPECT PRAISE**. Don't expect the receiving person to be thankful. A person with character gives a compliment because they mean it, not because they expect a reward.

5. **EXPECT SURPRISE**. Compliments sometimes embarrass, surprise, or confuse people. If they respond in an awkward fashion, then just move onto another topic. They may be insecure and need to think about the compliment before responding.

Accepting nice words

Accept a compliment with grace and humility not arrogance, distrust, or embarrassment.

A person who says nice words may or may not be currying favor with you. Time will tell if that is the case. Never publicly question the motives. That can be done in private if necessary.

TOP TIP
POWER EXISTS IN SHIFTING POSITIVE ATTENTION TO OTHER PEOPLE.

When accepting nice words....

1. **IT'S TRUE**. Don't try to dissuade the person from giving the compliment. That's calling them a liar. Simply thank them for their kindness.

2. **EMBARRASSMENT**. Try not to feel awkward or embarrassed when hearing a compliment. Don't reward kindness with uneasiness.

3. **HUMILITY**. A person with character receives a compliment by being humble, not arrogantly self-assured. Say "thank you" not "I know."

4. **ONE FOR ONE**. Don't respond by giving a compliment. That lessens the value of the first compliment. "Even things up" at a later date.

People usually give a compliment because they believe it's true and they want to tell another. A strong person figuratively bows down in gratitude to accept the kindness.

The appropriate response is to say "Thank you. That is very kind." Any further conversation makes the giver feel uncomfortable or the receiver look ungrateful or self-centered, and that defeats the purpose of the compliment.

One last warning to those accepting compliments: Be wary of people who use them to gain trust for personal gain. Many real-life examples tell of people who get duped, cheated, or worse by failing prey to silver-tongued predators.

Don't fall victim to unsolicited compliments from those who appeal to desires or weaknesses. As the saying goes, "If it sounds too good to be true, then it usually is."

The dangers of compliments

While saying or hearing nice words produces positive feelings, those words can be harmful, like too much powerful medicine causing an addiction.

Here are people who face the potential of compliment addiction:

1. **LEADERS**: Too much praise for leaders leads to poor decisions. People in charge begin to believe in compliments regarding their

infallible skills. Soon they seek self-aggrandizing solutions instead of searching for answers that serve the best interests of all. Failure soon follows.

2. **THE INSECURE**: Insecure individuals cling to kind words as they serve as a tonic to overcome insecurity. The need to hear kind words supersedes the need to achieve due to a lack of faith in their talent.

3. **THE NEEDY**: People who need compliments should step back and look within. Those looking to others for fulfillment will never be truly fulfilled.

4. **THE UNREALISTIC**: People lose sight of reality and need praise to keep up illusions. Dwell in reality and let illusions go.

5. **THE SUCCESSFUL**: Don't fall in love with the applause. It is a drug that prevents growth.

6. **THE VULNERABLE**: The unscrupulous use compliments to lure the vulnerable into traps. Guard against those who seek to take advantage by using kind words as bait for their trap.

Conclusion

Compliments serve as a tool to provide acknowledgment and encouragement to those who truly deserve it. Everyone enjoys a pat on the back for a superior effort and offering compliments in worthwhile situations makes the world a better place to live.

As an English-speaking tool, properly-used compliments show strength, humility, and kindness, all positive traits that build relationships and conversation.

Situation 4: Invitations

"A real conversation always involves an invitation. You are inviting another person to reveal himself or herself to you, to tell you who they are or what they want."

David Whyte

Invitations and conversations go hand in hand like a walk in the park on a sunny day. People invite because they want to talk, learn more about another person, and enjoy their company.

An invitation takes a budding relationship to the next level. Inviting another to explore common interest, share a meal, watch a movie, work on a project, or simply take a walk expresses a desire to open an ongoing dialogue. The invitation says "Let's talk and see where it leads."

This chapter discusses the importance of giving and receiving invitations and provides suggestions about how to handle the details.

Invitation: A spoken or written request to somebody to do something or to go somewhere.

A gift to a friend

Everyone loves to get a brightly wrapped gift. The sparkling wrapping paper and carefully tied bow promise a wonderful surprise within the hidden treasure.

View an invitation as a gift to a friend. The time, money, and effort expended to bring about the event serve as the present, so why not gaily wrap it up with kind words when giving the gift?

TOP TIP
INVITING A PERSON YOU DON'T KNOW WELL IS THE THIRD STEP IN RELATIONSHIP BUILDING. THE STEPS ARE:

1. Say hello and make a good first impression
2. Begin the process of making a friend through complimenting and asking questions
3. Extend an invitation for further friendship or business growth

What to do?

Giving a beautifully wrapped box with nothing inside won't win many friends. An invitation to spend time together with a friend without thoughtful planning brings the same results.

When inviting another have a plan or "gift" in mind. Ask yourself:

- What does the person like to do?
- When do they have free time?
- How well do I know them and how comfortable will we be spending time together?

TOP TIP
GIVE AN INVITATION WITH LOVING CARE. INVITING SOMEONE TO AN EVENT, DINNER, OR THE MOVIES BRINGS EXCITEMENT LIKE THE PRETTIEST WRAPPED GIFT.

Be open-minded about the invitation. A plan to go to the movies may become a dinner instead, but having a plan starts the ball rolling in the right direction.

Other points to keep in mind when inviting:

1. **DETAILS**. Be specific about what to do. Ask someone "Do you want to go to the movies on Saturday?" instead of "Do you want to hang out some time?"

2. **MORE DETAILS**. Provide information regarding the date, time and travel arrangements when finalizing the date.

3. **WHAT TO BRING.** Let them know what to bring such as money, a lunch, a gift, or a coat.

4. **TIME**. Give the guest or guests time between the invitation and the event to prepare, arrange schedules, or get permission; the more required of the invitee, the more time needed.

5. **NO IS OK**. People have the right say no so accept it with a smile. Don't make them feel guilty for refusing, whatever the reason. Guilt increases the chances that they'll always say no.

6. **FLEXIBILITY**. If inviting a group of people then try to accommodate as many as possible with suitable details such as time, date and location. Realize not everyone may be able to come so keep schedule juggling to a minimum.

7. **IN PRIVATE**. Don't invite guests in front of a person not invited. This makes the uninvited person feel bad and you look bad.

8. **DON'T HURT FEELINGS**. Avoid inviting people from a group of acquaintances and not others. This guarantees bad feelings among the uninvited, which makes good intentions appear cruel.

"I want to spend my life with people and do nice things and go on adventures, read books and have nice food and celebrate things. I don't want to spend the rest of my life in the bedroom like some people who just go to bed and never get out again."

Tracey Emin

Question of the day

Talk about the following question with a friend or form an opinion on your own. Read the conversation between Emmett, Iris and Edie and then consider how you would respond. Remember to explain your reasoning.

Question: Do you find it harder to say "no" or "yes" to an invitation?

- **Iris**: I'm shy. When people ask me to do something, I get tongue-tied and don't know what to say. Then my mind starts thinking about what we would talk about if I say yes, so I usually just make up an excuse and say no.
- **Emmett**: I always say yes because I don't want to hurt the feelings of the person asking me. But, sometimes, as soon as I say yes, I know I don't want to go. Then I feel bad and I don't know why.
- **Edie**: I have no problem saying no. If you do something you don't want to do then no one is happy. You feel bad for saying yes and your attitude shows it. Then the person who invited you gets upset. Nobody wins.

Which is harder? Saying yes or no?

Benefits beat rejection

Extending an invitation to another involves risk. The potential for rejection always exists so it takes strength and courage.

But the benefits far outweigh the potential downside because people usually invite others they find interesting, worthwhile, and important.

Accept the yinyang of the situation, balancing the fear of rejection with the benefits of enjoying the company. The benefits outweigh the sting of rejection so don't let the threat slow you down.

The benefits of inviting a person:

1. **GET TO KNOW PEOPLE.** Inviting an intriguing person for coffee to find out more about them may lead to friendship, business opportunities, or love. Invitations show interest and strength.
2. **LEARN ABOUT YOURSELF.** Talking to others who are not friends requires a person to open up. Having to reveal personal feelings results in surprises! A person may end up saying "I can't believe I said that about myself!"
3. **BEING SEEN.** Going out gets people seen by not only the guest but others in the community. That's never a bad thing.
4. **ACTION LEADS TO ACTION.** Life teaches us that action leads to more action. Meeting new people leads to more opportunities.

Action leads to action

Let's plan

Planning creates the best opportunity for a good time and stimulating conversation. Several planning considerations include:

1. **What do you want to do?** Talk? Exercise? Eat?
2. **Whom do you want to invite?** One, two, or many? Do certain people need to be there? Will people feel more comfortable if they bring a friend?
3. **What do you want to achieve?** A better relationship? Fun? Business? What's the best environment to reach your goal?
4. **When's the best time for the get together?** Morning, noon or night?
5. **What does the other person need for the event?** Generally the fewer requirements, the better the invitation.
6. **Are the time and/or location flexible?** Will you change if certain people cannot attend? Be open and attentive and not a slave to an agenda if possible.
7. **Where is the event?**
8. **How will people get to the event?**
9. **How long will it last?**
10. **How much will it cost?**

By knowing the answers to these questions before inviting others, you ensure an invitation's success. Remember being open to a wider range of thought produces more creative ideas. Don't do the ordinary!

Let's have fun

Suggestions on ways to have fun while practicing English:

- **Action activity:** Plan two activities using the planning questions above: one activity for you and one other person and one activity for a group of people. Be creative and fun!

- **Shared activity:** Talk to a creative friend or relative about your invitation ideas. Ask them for suggestions on improving the invitations.

- **Let's go somewhere:** Invite friends to a museum, a ballgame, or a festival, or ask them to come over to make sushi or any activity that sounds fun. Don't be discouraged if they can't make it. Just reschedule or ask another person or two.

Show character when invited

How a person responds to an invitation determines whether they receive a second invitation. Showing enthusiasm for an invitation makes the giving person glad and shows your character.

Shrugging your shoulders and saying "Oh, I guess I can come" sends a negative message to the person inviting you. Making others feel as if their invitation is a burden reveals poor manners and reduces the chances for future invitations. Refer to the "How to be likeable" section in the "Making friends" situation for tips.

An enthusiastic "yes"

Enthusiasm over an invitation sets the tone for an enjoyable experience. If you appear truly excited then the person inviting you will be excited as well.

Here are a few ways to say yes that make a person feel good about their decision to invite you.

- "That would be great."
- "I'd love to."

- "Sure. It sounds fun."
- "That's a wonderful idea."
- "Yes. When can we do it?"

If you're going to say yes, then why not do it with enthusiasm? If not, then just say no and don't waste everyone's time.

When having to say no...

Saying no to a request takes skill and strength of character. People ask you to do things because they think highly of you. Don't take that thoughtfulness lightly.

But sometimes we must say "no thank you." Many reasons exist why people say no. This book won't judge good reasons or bad reasons to reject an invitation or request. Just remember no one likes rejection, so be tactful in refusing an invitation. Thoughts on saying no:

1. **NO**. Look someone in the eye to give them a firm no. Mumbling an excuse or hesitating appears deceitful or indecisive, showing weakness and a lack of character. Apologize for the inability to attend. Only go into the details for a refusal if necessary. Otherwise, "I'm sorry my schedule doesn't permit it" suffices.
2. **NO WITH REASON**. Telling someone no may require a lighter touch than a direct no. Using phrases such as "I would love to go but…" "I need to focus on…" or "I can't believe I am unavailable…"
3. **YES BUT NO**. Don't lead someone on by saying yes when you know it won't happen. This rude action lacks courage. People would rather hear the truth.
4. **ENCOURAGE THE OTHER PERSON**. Always give a person

positive feedback for an invitation. Thank them for their invitation and kindness in thinking of you.

5. **REMAIN FIRM**. People try all sorts of ways to change people's minds. Three common methods include sweet talk, pressure, and complaining. Show personal strength by not allowing others to weaken your resolve, while remaining polite.

6. **REMAIN OPEN TO FUTURE INVITATIONS**. Depending upon the person and the situation, keep an open mind about future invitations. Leaving them with a "Please keep me in mind the next time" ends conversations in a positive way.

"The art of leadership is saying no, not saying yes. It is very easy to say yes."

Tony Blair, former British prime minister

Responding to an invitation

Today's world allows for a number of ways to give and receive invitations. Invitations come by:

- Mail
- E-mail
- Social media sites like Facebook
- Telephone
- In person
- Pebbles thrown at a window by a messenger

Ways to properly respond to an invitation:

1. **RSVP**. French: Répondez s'il vous plaît (Respond if you please, or please reply). This request asks for a response on whether you will be able to accept the invitation. Mailed and e-mailed invitations often have an RSVP request form asking you to let the host know your availability. Respond to the request, either yes or no, by the RSVP date.

2. **KEEP YOUR WORD**. If you say yes then do your best to go. Avoid changing your mind at the last minute without warning. Most consider this rude.

3. **ASK FOR TIME**. Face-to-face invitations or telephone requests can be difficult. If you are not sure, then say "I'm not sure I can make it. Can I let you know?" Make sure to let them know as soon as possible. Ignoring or hiding from them to avoid responding shows weakness and a lack of character.

Conversation: Giving an invitation

Notice how Sam and Spike first make small talk before asking the girls to the movies. They know the details of the movie time but remain flexible on changing the date to accommodate Snow and Sunshine. Practice emphasis.

Sam and Spike walk into a local restaurant and see Snow and Sunshine seated in a booth having lunch. They want to ask them to go to the movies.

Sam: _Hey,_ girls. _What_ are you having for lunch?

Snow: Oh, hello, Sam. Hello, Spike. Good to _see_ you two. You remember _Sunshine_ don't you?

Sam: Of _course_. How've you _been,_ Sunshine? How was your trip to the beach together?

Sunshine: _Great_ except for the jellyfish that _stung_ me while we were swimming. That _hurt_.

Spike: Yikes. Are you OK _now_? I know how much those sting.

Sunshine: Sure, I'm fine. Are you two _here_ with someone? You can _join_ us if you want.

Sam: No, thanks. We were walking by and _saw_ you two through the window. Remember we talked about _going_ to the movies together. I want to know if you two would like to go _next_ Friday night with us. The movie _starts_ at 7:00 pm at the Aeon Mall. It's a really _scary_ Halloween movie that opens Friday.

Snow: Hmmm. Let me _think_. Oh, yeah, I am _babysitting_ Friday night. So, I _can't_ go. What about _Saturday_ instead?

Spike: That _works_ for Sam and me. We're _always_ looking for things to do.

Sunshine: I'd like to go, but I am not a _fan_ of spooky movies. You guys can go _without_ me.

Sam: Nooo. Come _on_. Nothing bad will happen.

Snow: Can we see _another_ movie? I am not crazy about scary movies _either_.

Spike: Sure. We can _meet_ you two at the theater at 6:30 pm and decide then which movie to see. We can all buy our _own_ tickets. Is that _OK_?

Sunshine: Works for _me_. If anything changes, give one of us a call. Bye.

Sam and Spike: Goodbye.

No fear

The two biggest fears regarding invitations involve the possibility of refusal or acceptance. Keep these points in mind.

1. **PEOPLE SAY NO**. People refuse invitations every day. Accept the refusal with a smile not a frown. The effort makes you a kind person. Using sarcasm or anger when refused reveals an unattractive side to you that guarantees further rejections.

2. **PEOPLE SAY YES**. People saying yes to an invitation can be as scary as no. A yes requires the host to make sure the person or people enjoy themselves. A lack of preparation reflects poor planning, indecision, and weakness.

3. **KEEP ASKING**. Stay strong by continuing to invite after rejection.

4. **ENOUGH ALREADY**. Move on from people who always refuse invitations. Show strength by not taking it personally, and understand that everyone has the right to say no. If you never expect results, then you will never be disappointed.

Don't delay

Invitations create as much angst in life as giving a speech in public. A person can fret for weeks or months over giving or receiving an invitation for a cup of coffee. That's a big waste of time and energy.

Invitations are like emotions. If you allow them to overwhelm then they cause excessive and unnecessary torment that harm a person's ability to communicate.

Seek balance when dealing with the uncertainty of an invitation. Don't dwell exclusively in the potential of rejection (if asking) or the message accepting or rejecting sends (if asked). Keep the positive sides in mind as well.

Consider the options involved and deal with the invitation as soon as possible. Letting it linger lets the uncertainty boil inside you like an acid, hurting you not the other person. Deal with it quickly so it doesn't continue to bother you. You'll feel much better.

Don't let invitations build up to be bigger than they need to be. Either extend an invitation or respond to one without delay and move on with life.

Conclusion

Life is much more fun when enjoying it with other people. Invitations serve as the means for making that happen.

Don't let the fear of rejection stop you from enjoying life. That gives others power over you.

And don't say no to an invitation just because the unknown makes you a little nervous. Life's mysteries often produce amazing results.

Situation 5: Presentations

I stand frozen as full panic mode takes over my mind and body. Twenty-five people stare at me with looks of bewilderment. My shoulders droop like two ice-covered tree branches as my trembling, ice-cold hands hold a notecard with unreadable words. I try to speak but soft squeaky sounds come out instead. Oh my god, people are giggling! My face turns a bright crimson red. I want to die. I hate giving presentations!

Surveys show that speaking in front of people ranks as North Americans' number one fear. Death ranks number two!

The fear of speaking in public is called *glossophobia*. Almost every person alive suffers from its symptoms. Shy, foreign and frustrated English speakers are usually at the top of the list.

Shaky nerves

Typical nerve-wracking situations include class presentations, dinner speeches, public ceremonies, assemblies, and work settings.

This chapter looks for relief from the jitters and provides common-sense ways to overcome public speaking fear.

Why does speaking in public scare a person? Simply put, the act requires a brave soul.

A speech requires a person to stand and expose insecurities in front of uncaring strangers. The audience stands as judge and jury of the speaker's brains, looks, voice, and clothes. No wonder one worries "What if I look stupid?"

Five nervous reasons

A speaker gets jittery for the following reasons:

1. The fear of failure
2. Expecting to be perfect
3. A perceived lack of skills or knowledge
4. Uncontrolled emotions
5. Unfamiliar situations

Shaky? It's OK!

Speakers try to calm down before speaking to an audience. They sit quietly, telling themselves that they'll be fine. But, as soon as they face the audience, they fall apart.

You'll likely forget these reasons not to be nervous the next time you give a pubic presentation but we'll give them anyway!

Six reasons not to worry about giving a speech:

1. Everybody gets nervous speaking in public.
2. The audience expects you to be nervous.
3. The audience can rarely tell if someone's nervous.
4. The audience wants the speaker to succeed.
5. The audience doesn't know what to expect. If the speech comes out differently than planned, only the speaker knows.
6. Surveys show that only 20 percent of an audience actually listens at any one time.

It's OK to be nervous but realize most won't be able to tell, want you to succeed, and probably aren't listening!

TOP TIP
DON'T BE ASHAMED OF BEING A NERVOUS SPEAKER. NERVES SHOW YOU CARE AND WANT TO DO WELL. THAT'S POSITIVE! SHAKY? IT'S OK!

Speeches and presentations: The basics

Let's look at the practical aspects of talking in front of people.

1. **DON'T TRY TOO HARD**. Trying too hard creates negative effects. Public speakers who try too hard to be super intelligent, funny, or thoughtful leave the opposite impression. Relax and let the speech flow naturally.

2. **CLARITY IS DIFFICULT**. An excellent public speaker strives for clarity. Unfortunately, what seems clear to the speaker often eludes the audience. Avoid jargon, obscure references, complex vocabulary, and acronyms when speaking. Don't assume an audience knows much about a topic. Err on the side of simplicity instead of complexity.

3. **BE OPEN-MINDED**. A wider range of thought produces creativity. Look at things backwards, upside-down, and inside-out when preparing. Push the audience to look at your subject in a new, easy-to-understand light.

4. **ACCEPT OUTCOME**. The saying "If you are not afraid of dying, then there is nothing you can't achieve" applies to public speaking. Fear disappears by accepting the outcome *before* the speech. This attitude frees the spirit, allowing the speaker to soar to new heights.

5. **CHANNEL ENERGY**. Channel your excess jitters into the speech. Turn nervous energy into excitement and the audience will love it. Examples of using nerves to your benefit include walking instead of standing at a podium, using a "big" voice at the beginning to capture attention, or excessive but planned body language. Using up excess energy calms you down.

Practice, practice, practice

Preparation makes a world of difference when giving a speech. Great ways to train for a speech include:

1. Practicing in front of a mirror.
2. Adding facial expressions and hand gestures.
3. Having friends listen to the speech.
4. Running the speech through your head quietly.
5. Practicing without notes.
6. Visualizing giving the speech in front of a cheering audience.

Don't practice saying a speech; practice *giving* a speech. This includes saying thank you to key people, hand and facial gestures, emphasized words, and pauses.

Let's have fun

Suggestions on ways to have fun while practicing English:

- **Action activity:** Research "great speeches" online and find videos of well-done speeches or interviews. Watch carefully for how to use words to build support for a case. Find three things excellent speakers do, such as the use of emphasis, hand gestures, the use of pauses, the use of voice tone and volume, or methods of getting the audience to agree.

- **Shared activity:** Ask a friend or relative about hearing or giving a great speech. Why was the speech effective? How did the audience react? What did the speaker do to capture the audience's attention?

- **Let's go somewhere:** Make an appointment with an active speaker such as a local public official like a mayor, a university professor, or a religious leader. Prepare a few questions on how they prepare and the important points in speaking to an audience.

Don't insult the audience

I'll be honest. I usually HATE listening to speeches. Too many speakers try so hard to convince the audience that the words not only fail to achieve the purpose but create the opposite effect.

Many speakers imply that anyone who does not agree with their premise must be wrong. This tactic does not convince the audience but usually chases them to the other side of the argument.

Let the audience disagree, question, or see where they fit into the discussion when giving a presentation. Let them judge whether the words and ideas are persuasive or not. Don't insult people's intelligence by pushing views too hard.

If the speech is persuasive, then chances are good they'll be right there with you at the end.

The audience-torture ranking

Even with the very best intentions, many poor or unfocused speakers torture unsuspecting audiences. Issues include long-winded speakers, repeating ideas, appearing unprepared, or using a monotone voice.

MY TOP TEN WORST SPEECH MISTAKES

1. A long speech read word-for-word.
2. A 100-slide PowerPoint presentation with a font size so small that most can't see the words so the speaker reads every slide.
3. A long, memorized monotone speech.
4. A drunk person with a microphone at a wedding. (No, don't say it!)
5. An angry speaker at a public meeting who starts by saying "I just have a few things to say" (guaranteed 20-minute-minimum unfocused rant with the same ideas repeated over and over).
6. A person preaching controversial views to an unsuspecting audience.
7. Blatant sales pitch without any redeeming benefits.
8. A poorly researched speech.
9. Unfunny speakers who think they're hilarious.
10. An intelligent person showing off by speaking above the audience.

Notice that nervous speakers do not appear on the list. We've been listening to nervous speeches all our lives. Audiences want nervous speakers to succeed.

Styles of speeches

Many politicians and actors give televised speeches with the aid of a teleprompter. The teleprompter allows them to read the entire speech word for word, including prompts for hand gestures, facial expressions, and pauses while looking at the audience.

Most people never give a speech using a teleprompter. Common folks deliver speeches in one of six old-fashioned ways:

1. An impromptu talk (a talk without preparing)
2. Memorizing a written speech
3. Reading a written speech
4. Using a PowerPoint presentation
5. Using a speech outline
6. Some combination of the above

Pros and cons of each style

Knowing the pros and cons of each speech style assists in deciding which one to use. A few thoughts on each speech style:

- **IMPROMPTU:** An unprepared speech used for short talks or certain English tests. A surprise request to speak can catch you off guard but there are advantages. Speaking without notes allows for audience eye contact and a more genuine talk. Inexperienced speakers must beware a longer speech without notes can become like a walk in the forest at night where retracing steps, meandering, and hitting dead ends leave the speaker and the audience lost. Keep it short and if you hit a spot when the audience laughs or applauds then sit down.
- **MEMORIZED SPEECH:** Memorizing a speech takes too long and allows for the possibility of forgetting key points. Only skilled speakers can memorize a speech while effectively using

gestures, expressions, and emphasis without appearing mechanical. Inexperienced speakers who memorize a speech focus on recall, appearing robotic. People who give the same speech over and over lose effectiveness due to familiarity. Try to keep it fresh.

- **READING A SPEECH:** *Please* don't read a speech word for word off pieces of paper. The cruelest and most boring act a human does to other humans involves reading a long speech.

"PowerPoint makes us stupid."

James Mattis

- **POWERPOINT PRESENTATIONS:** PowerPoint presentations (Ppts) come in a close second on the audience-torturing scale. Slides look alike after a few minutes; the audience gets bored and the level of enthusiasm in the room sinks to that of watching paint dry. The worst PowerPoint presentations use small type in front of a large audience. Even interested audience members cannot see the slides and become bored or disappointed.

  Slides can be useful in bringing home points, but mix it up with other techniques such as questions, humor, real-life examples, and physical movement. Demonstrate; don't explain.
- **NOTECARDS:** Using 3 x 5 notecards with major points and a few ideas to keep the speaker on track makes the most sense, especially when mixing in a joke, slides, and movement. Notecards allow for improvisation, questions, or new wrinkles.

The politician's trick

No one speaks more than political leaders. They give both prepared talks and impromptu discussions to small groups, the news media, and supporters.

What can you do if required to give an unprepared talk at work, school, or a speech contest?

Politicians use a valuable trick when asked to make a short, unprepared talk involving the use of a transition or bridge. The speaker takes the subject of the question and transitions to a topic they want to discuss.

An example: A news reporter asks a politician about raising taxes to build better roads. The politician says:

"Thanks for the great question. I support better roads because they help the economy grow (the transition which doesn't discuss higher taxes). I've been working on a plan to bring more jobs to our region by introducing new legislation...(the topic the politician wishes to discuss). The economic benefit of the legislation includes increased employment and money for new roads which will become important in achieving a better local economy with lower, not higher, taxes. I hope that answers your question."

This style of answering questions gives the speaker the ability to discuss a topic they know instead of one they may be unfamiliar with or is politically dangerous.

The key is taking the question, leading it to what you want to talk about or what you know and then finish by referring back to the original question or topic.

11 steps to a mistake-free speech

Want to give a mistake-free speech? Follow these simple steps in giving great presentations.

1. **RESEARCH**. Do a thorough job researching the topic. ALWAYS choose comfortable and familiar topics. Audiences can spot phonies who talk about unfamiliar topics.
2. **MORE RESEARCH**. Research the audience before speaking. Who in the audience and what do they want to hear? How much knowledge or interest do they have regarding the speech topic?
3. **IT'S ALL ABOUT THE AUDIENCE**. The audience provides the reason for a presentation. No audience, no presentation. Treat the audience with respect. Entertain and educate them!
4. **START WRITING**. Write the entire speech word for word. Make sure to have a very strong beginning and ending.
5. **PRACTICE, PRACTICE, PRACTICE**. Practice the word-for-word speech so you know it very well.
6. **OUTLINE IT**. Outline the complete speech by writing major points and a few ideas for each point. Write down specific sentences that need to be said but limit them.
7. **GESTURES, PAUSES, EXPRESSIONS**: Don't forget to put in the outline appropriate places to make a gesture or pause.
8. **3 X 5 IT**. Write the outline on 3 x 5 notecards.
9. **3 X 5 PRACTICE**. Practice, practice, practice giving the speech using the 3 x 5 card outline. Keep the cards and speech at the same place (even if you're not using the cards) in case you need to refer to the outline.
10. **AUTHENTIC**. Be authentic when giving the speech. Accept yourself and the audience will accept you. Don't try to act like

an esteemed Rhodes Scholar if you're an everyday kind of person. People sense and appreciate honesty. They also appreciate speakers who are like them.

11. **ENJOY THE SPEECH**. Give the speech with a sense of joy. Don't dread the experience; embrace it. Again, accept the outcome *before* the speech and channel nervous energy into the speech.

The mistake-free technique provides freedom to leave a few words out or to add a few along the way. This flexibility allows last-minute additions or subtractions if something changes. Remember the audience never heard the speech so they have no idea what is "right" or "wrong."

A speech built this way comes across like a conversation with a friend, which builds rapport.

Don't go overboard with hand gestures or facial expressions, but know where they belong in the speech, delivering them on cue along with good eye contact.

Clarity: The speech-writing goal

The old adage about writing a speech says, "Tell the audience what you're going to say, tell them, and then tell them what you said." This process focuses on clarity.

Clarity is difficult to achieve. What seems obvious or clear can confuse an audience. Avoid complex words, acronyms, and jargon. Instead of conveying a point of view in a boring monologue, focus on telling a story.

TOP TIP
TELL THE AUDIENCE A STORY INSTEAD OF "GIVING A SPEECH."

The basic outline for a speech or presentation:

1. **THE CRITICAL BEGINNING**. A strong start to a speech is critical. A speaker engages or loses an audience in the first few words. Six ways to start a speech:

   - Humor
   - A story or anecdote
   - A question
   - A startling fact
   - Silence
   - A relevant quotation

   A speech topic lends itself to one or more of these openings. Statistics show getting an audience to smile or laugh at the beginning of a speech significantly increases the likelihood they will enjoy the presentation. But be careful, no jokes in serious situations and definitely no tasteless, sexist, racist, or crude jokes or comments.

2. **TELL THEM**. Next, tell the audience the speech in a condensed fashion such as, "Tonight's talk centers on the importance of music in the world of politics."

3. **MAIN TOPICS**. Then tell them about the topic using no more than 3-4 main points.

4. **REPEAT**. Finish by summarizing the 3-4 main points.

5. **WRAP UP**. Conclude by referring to the beginning joke or opening tactic (fact, quote, etc.) and then drive home the conclusion in a humorous, forceful, or dramatic fashion.

6. **THANK THE AUDIENCE**.

Crazy ways to calm down

Giving presentations make the bravest people anxious, so it's OK to get nervous. How to calm down before the speech depends on what works for you. Sometimes the solution may be crazier than being nervous. Check out these mad ways to face fear.

1. Un-tense your body by pretending to be made of rubber.
2. Before the speech, collapse on the ground like a limp doll.
3. Lie on the ground or sit in a chair, close your eyes, and act like you're floating in space.
4. Stand 18 inches away from a wall and push against it with the palms of your hands. Breathe out, contracting your stomach muscles like rowing a boat.
5. Give the speech to only a few faces in the audience. Make eye contact with them and feel as if you're talking at a coffee shop.
6. Give as many speeches as possible. The more you do something, the less scary it becomes.
7. Before the speech look into a mirror and use your lips to laugh like a horse.
8. When starting, tell the audience you're nervous. Admitting problems helps to solve them.
9. Put on headphones and listen to your favorite music prior to the speech.
10. A few minutes before the speech stand like your favorite superhero …tall, strong, and unafraid. When you begin, take that same pose.

Question of the day

Talk about the following question with a friend and form an opinion. Read the conversation between Emmett, Iris and Edie and then consider how you would respond. Remember to explain your reasons.

Question: What can you do to calm down before a speech?

- **Emmett**: I get really nervous before a speech in front of any more than two people. What works for me is to exercise before the talk. If I go for a short run, ride my bicycle, or just go for a walk, my body calms down. Then just before talking, I take three or four really deep breaths.
- **Iris**: That doesn't always work if speaking in the middle of the day. I try to visualize giving the speech by closing my eyes and seeing myself talking in front of everyone. I visualize the room, audience, and speech. I see people smiling and clapping. I know that it sounds strange, but it works for me.
- **Edie**: Nothing works for me. I just try to work through the speech the best I can. I focus on my opening so that it is solid. If I start strong then the speech goes better. If I flub the beginning then it is usually all downhill.

What do you do before speaking in front of an audience? Do you think Emmett, Iris, or Edie has the best technique for calming down?

"I must not fear. Fear is the mind-killer. Fear is the little-death that brings total obliteration. I will face my fear. I will permit it to pass over me and through me. And when it has gone past I will turn the inner eye to see its path. When the fear has gone there will be nothing. Only I will remain."

Frank Herbert, *Dune*

Motivational talks: Famous examples

Movies and politics provide sensational examples of motivational speeches. While movie actors have many chances to nail a scene, the best performers show the passion required to deliver a powerful message. Politicians speak in incredibly emotional environments that multiply the impact of the spoken word.

Here are two examples of motivational speeches, one with an actor and one with a politician.

ROCKY 4: Actor Sylvester Stallone plays aging fighter Rocky Balboa in *Rocky 4*. Rocky is an absent father who talks to his son about how hard life can be. See how the writer sets up the speech in a very simple but effective way.

"Let me tell you something you already know. The world ain't all sunshine and rainbows. It is a very mean and nasty place and I don't care how tough you are, it will beat you to your knees and keep you there permanently if you let it. You, me, or nobody is gonna hit as hard as life.

"But it ain't about how hard you hit; it's about how hard you can get hit and keep moving forward. It's how much you can take, and keep moving forward. That's how winning is done.

"Now, if you know what you're worth, then go out and get what you're worth. But you gotta be willing to take the hits, and not point fingers and blame other people. Cowards do that and that ain't you. You're better than that!"

147

THE GETTYSBURG ADDRESS: US President Abraham Lincoln gave one of the most famous inspirational speeches in American history, focusing on freedom, its costs, and responsibilities.

"Four score and seven years ago our fathers brought forth on this continent, a new nation, conceived in liberty, and dedicated to the proposition that all men are created equal.

"Now we are engaged in a great civil war, testing whether that nation, or any nation so conceived and so dedicated, can long endure. We are met on a great battlefield of that war. We have come to dedicate a portion of that field, as a final resting place for those who here gave their lives that that nation might live. It is altogether fitting and proper that we should do this.

"But in a larger sense, we cannot dedicate — we cannot conse-crate — we cannot hallow — this ground. The brave men, living and dead, who struggled here, have consecrated it, far above our poor power to add or detract. The world will little note, nor long remember, what we say here, but it can never forget what they did here. It is for us the living, rather, to be dedicated here to the unfinished work which they who fought here have thus far so nobly advanced. It is rather for us to be here dedicated to the great task remaining before us — that from these honored dead we take increased devotion to that cause for which they gave the last full measure of devotion — that we here highly resolve that these dead shall not have died in vain — that this nation, under God, shall have a new birth of freedom — and that government of the people, by the people, for the people, shall not perish from the earth."

"Life is finite, while knowledge is infinite."

Conclusion

Speaking in public is tough. I've done it thousands of time but still get a little nervous before a talk starts. I've learned to channel that nervous energy into the speech by smiling, moving, and using a loud voice.

That works for me, but everyone needs to find their own tricks to balance their emotions. If you give enough public talks then an answer will come to you.

My final points to the nervous speakers:

- Preparation and practice set the tone
- Nerves will be present so acknowledge them
- Accept the outcome before the talk
- Critique your performance, refining your skills for the next speech

Situation 6: Talking and eating

The important business lunch made me nervous. I sat across from a powerful, stone-faced businessman in an Athens, Ohio restaurant. We both ordered a cup of soup and a cup of coffee, which the waitress brought within minutes. She served the soup in a cup with a handle much like a coffee cup. Picking up a container of cream for the coffee, I mistakenly poured it into my soup. My face turned beet red with embarrassment. Instead of simply admitting my nervous mistake, I picked up a spoon, stirred the cream

**into the soup, and ate it while talking to my startled guest.
He just shook his head.**

Talking and eating go together like babies and crying. Every day people share food while talking about business, love, family, politics, sports, art, and the weather. This chapter focuses on how to be a positive force during a meal.

Food, conversation, character....

Let's start with basic dinner manners. How people eat exposes character and culture. Jobs, relationships, and business deals can implode due to poor manners or cultural mistakes while sharing food.

Many people erroneously think: *What's wrong with the way I eat?* The fact is, we eat so often that repetition deeply engrains bad habits. Then one day an important dinner meeting exposes our shortcoming, causing embarrassment.

Keep the basics in mind while talking during a meal:

1. **EMPTY MOUTH**. Don't talk with food in the mouth. Remember:
   a.) Food in mouth
   b.) Chew with mouth closed
   c.) Swallow
   d.) Talk
   e.) Repeat.
2. **EXCUSE ME**. When leaving the table for any reason, simply say, "Excuse me. I'll be right back." No explanation is required, but it is rude to leave without saying anything.
3. **NO CELL**. Put cellphones on vibrate. The prevalent form of rudeness in the 21st century involves texting, talking on the phone, or

surfing the Internet while eating with others. Leave the table to take necessary calls but keep them to a strict minimum (See Number 2). This includes people who think they are very important.

4. **UTENSILS DOWN**. Properly chew and swallow food and put the utensil(s) down or hold them at table level when wishing to speak. Don't point forks, knives, spoons, or chopsticks like weapons while talking.

TOP TIP
PEOPLE REVEAL MANNERS, EMOTIONS, AND ATTITUDE WHEN EATING. WHAT DO YOU REVEAL?

5. **MENU DOWN**. Close the menu and place it on the table when ready to order food in a restaurant.

6. **MANNERS AND OTHER CULTURES**. When eating with a guest from another culture, make sure you are aware of particular manners from that culture. Ask or research if necessary.

7. **MMMMM, THAT WAS DELICIOUS**. When eating at someone's home compliment them on well-prepared food.

8. **HEY YOU**....To inform another of food on the face get their attention by silently pointing to the spot where the food is located.

9. **ONE**. Do one thing at a time. When eating, chew and swallow before talking. When talking, don't eat. When drinking, swallow then talk.

10. **NO FIGHTS**. Avoid disagreeable conversations, especially when dining with a number of people. People want to enjoy their meals, not get into a fight.

11. **WAIT**. Don't start eating until all people have been served food.

12. **TABLE SETTING**. Know the function for each utensil, plate and glass when seated at a formal dinner.
13. **SLOWLY ENJOY THE MEAL**. Chefs don't give prizes for the fastest eaters. Appreciate the food and the conversation.

**"Everyone eats and drinks;
yet only a few appreciate the taste of food."**

The scary dinner table

The dinner table creates scary scenes. My father used to rap me on the head with his fork at the dinner table when he disagreed with my spirited comments or actions. Now the knock didn't do any damage but it was an effective way to get my attention. Doing that to a child today, however, could get you arrested.

Hopefully no physical violence occurs in your dining life. But verbal thwacks happen all the time. Challenging conversations make eating dinner a difficult proposition.

Dinner table conversations trap us like a rabbit in a cage whether it's a large hotel ballroom dinner with lots of strangers, a tense business luncheon, or a family holiday celebration. You can't run away so you have to handle the challenge.

Talking tips while eating

The best tip involves planning the dinner conversation. Preparing things to say for an upcoming dinner helps control the dialogue.

1. **ASK QUESTIONS**. People love to talk about themselves, so ask nonthreatening queries to keep dining guests occupied. Questions about vacations, holidays, family, and pets keep things light and easy.
2. **TALK ABOUT MOVIES/TV SHOWS**. Current films and TV shows make excellent time-killing topics.
3. **ACTIVE LISTENING**. Listen to what fellow diners say, and then when they stop, rephrase their comments into a question. "So you went to the concert last weekend. Wow. How often do you go to concerts?" Sit back, listen, and continue eating.
4. **SILENCE**. Silence serves as a great source of strength. Don't feel that pithy comments need to fill every second. Silence serves as a delightful second course.
5. **UNIQUE TOPICS**. New inventions, foreign cultures, odd historical events, strange news, or time travel serve as a few examples of themes that break up monotonous dinners. Just be careful not to go too far out on a limb like asking Grandma her favorite rap singer.

The guerrilla commander's six dining strategies

Bad history can flare up when dining with others. Unresolved arguments, past resentments, or petty jealousies spring out of the weeds like a surprise attack. Using the Guerrilla Commander's Six Dining Strategies repels the dining invaders.

TOP TIP
RELAX, PLAN, AND USE INTELLIGENCE WHEN FACING DIFFICULT DINING EXPERIENCES.

A guerrilla commander knows attacks happen without warning. Having a defined strategy to follow in any hostile circumstance reduces costly errors in the battlefield or at the dinner table.

THE GUERRILLA COMMANDER'S SIX DINING STRATEGIES

1. **DON'T SEEK A FIGHT**. A commander tries to fight on his or her terms. If a surprise attack takes place at the dinner table, then yield and step back. Don't go stumbling into a battle you're not prepared to wage.

Don't seek a fight

2. **INTELLIGENCE.** Your best weapon is intelligence.

Intelligence: The ability to acquire and apply knowledge

Apply your intelligence of dining partners to steer conversations to safer grounds. When a sticky situation arises, gently direct the conversation to less-volatile topics that the dining partner enjoys. Use your intelligence to avoid problems.

3. **ADVANCING.** The guerrilla commander only advances when not opposed. Don't try to fight through resistance if introducing material at the dinner table that has potential for conflict unless you agreed to discuss it prior to the meeting.

4. **STEP BACK**. If you unintentionally hit potential trouble, then immediately step back. Don't overstep the invisible boundaries that exist in every conversation.

Step back

5. **DON'T CLING TO SUCCESS**. Don't cling to a successful point in a conversation. A savvy commander gets in and gets out. If the conversation goes well, then move on instead of running it into the ground.

6. **RESPECT THE ATTACKER**. The guerrilla commander always respects his or her attacker. Making light or disparaging remarks about a dinner partner creates a risk so avoid unnecessary slights.

The key elements to the Guerrilla Commander's Six Dining Strategies involve intelligence, guile, and calm under fire. Keep them close at hand when a surprise attack occurs while dining.

Let's have fun

Suggestions on ways to have fun while practicing English:

- **Action activity:** Test your skills by having dinner with a difficult relative or acquaintance. Plan the conversation and prepare Guerrilla Commander Dining Strategies regarding your dining partner. Where is he or she likely to attack? What intelligence do you have? How can you sidestep issues? Critique the performance and determine whether more work is necessary.

- **Shared activity:** Ask a friend or relative about a difficult dinner conversation they have had. What made them feel bad or uncomfortable? Did they handle it well or not?

- **Let's go somewhere:** Plan a lunch or dinner date with a group of friends. Plan the meal's discussion topics without telling the others. Set the date and see if you can direct the conversation by interjecting topics as situations allow. Don't be pushy. Review the dinner, noting good and bad points in the conversation.

Conversation: At a restaurant

Notice how Snow asks a question to start the conversation and avoids getting into an argument with Spike over the movie. See how emphasis makes Spike's words rude.

Snow, Sunshine, Sam and Spike get together for pizza after the movie.

Snow: What did _you_ guys think of the movie?

Sunshine: I _enjoyed_ the movie. The star was _so_ handsome.

Snow: Yes, he was a _doll_. What about _you,_ Sam? Did _you_ like it?

Sam: Ah it was _OK_. Some parts were a little _too_ romantic, but the _ending_ was a surprise.

Spike: I thought it was a movie made for _girls_. Really _stupid_ and _boring_ and I don't see how _anyone_ could like it. I wanted to go to the _Halloween_ movie.

Snow: I _know,_ Spike. _Thanks_ for agreeing to go to this movie. _You_ can pick next time. What kind of movies do _you_ like?

Spike: Science fiction and superhero movies. Now _those_ rock.

Sunshine: Superhero movies _are_ cool. _Who's_ your favorite?

Spike: Wolverine.

Sam: _Mine_ is Spiderman. I'd love to _crawl_ up the side of a building.

Sunshine: What about _you,_ Snow?

Snow: I like movies about strong women.

Sam: What's your favorite movie?

Snow: _Wonder_ Woman!

Difficult food words

Making a soufflé requires mixing up ingredients. Ordering a soufflé doesn't require mixing up the pronunciation!

Common food words challenge English speakers since many come from other languages. French, German, Asian, Greek, and Spanish food words find their way onto restaurant menus throughout the world.

Embarrassing situations at a restaurant or dinner table involve butchering the pronunciation of food words. People avoid the problem by not ordering a dish because they don't know how to properly say the name. I know I have.

Let's work on eating what we want.

Restaurants

Visiting a foreign restaurant doesn't need to be a threatening experience. A few tips on ordering any item on a menu.

1. **PREPARE**: If possible, take a minute to check a restaurant's menu online before going to dinner. This allows you to be familiar with the choices.
2. **PRACTICE**: Look up the pronunciation of any unfamiliar words and practice them. Then impress a date or business client by precisely rattling off several foreign-named menu items when at the restaurant.

3. **ASK**: Don't try if the word is unfamiliar. The act can make you look foolish. Ask the waiter or those at the table how to pronounce it then practice it with everyone.

The Food Word Challenge

The Food Word Challenge tests knowledge about types of food and how to pronounce them.

Take the test by describing the foods below and pronouncing the names. Check the definition and pronunciation below.

Bruschetta	Worcestershire	Quinoa
Gyro	Pho	Gnocchi
Bouillabaisse	Espresso	Chipotle
Niçoise	Quesadilla	Açaí
Caprese	Foie-Gras	Endive
Macaron	Maraschino	Paella
Prosciutto	Poke	Baguette
Croissant	Crème brûlée	Coq au vin
Chorizo al vino	Jiaozi	Empanada
Huevos rancheros	Ceviche	Arroz con pollo
Frijoles	Ramen	Sashimi
Andouille	Étouffée	Soufflé

1. **BRUSCHETTA** *(Broo-SKET-uh)* Toasted bread with garlic and olive oil

2. **WORCESTERSHIRE** *(WOOH-stuh-shur)* Pungent sauce whose ingredients include soy, vinegar, and garlic

3. **QUINOA** *(KEEN-wa)* A gluten-free, whole-grain carbohydrate,

as well as a whole protein found in the Andes and cultivated for its edible starchy seeds

4. **GYRO** *(YEER-oh)* Greek dish made of meat, traditionally pork or chicken, cooked on a vertical rotisserie

5. **PHO** *(fuh)* Vietnamese soup, typically made from beef stock and spices to which noodles and thinly sliced beef or chicken are added

6. **GNOCCHI** *(nyohk-KEE)* (in Italian cooking) Small dumplings made from potato, semolina, or flour, usually served with a sauce

7. **BOUILLABAISSE** *(boo-YAH-base)* Rich, spicy stew or soup made with various kinds of fish, originally from Provence

8. **ESPRESSO** *(es-press-OH)* Strong black coffee made by forcing steam through ground coffee beans

9. **CHIPOTLE** *(chip-OAT-lay)* Smoked hot chili pepper used especially in Mexican cooking

10. **NIÇOISE** *(NEE-swazz)* Salad made of tomatoes, hard-boiled eggs, Niçoise olives, and anchovies, dressed with olive oil

11. **QUESADILLA** *(ke-suh-DEE-yah)* A tortilla filled with cheese and heated

12. **AÇAÍ** *(ah-sigh-EE)* South American palm tree producing small edible blackish-purple berries

13. **CAPRESE** *(cuh-PRAY-zah)* Salad of fresh mozzarella, tomatoes, and basil

14. **ENDIVE** *(ON-deev)* Edible Mediterranean plant whose bitter leaves may be blanched and used in salads

15. **FOIE-GRAS** *(FWAH-grah)* The liver of a specially fattened goose or duck prepared as food

16. **MACARON** *(mack-uh-HRON)* Small round cake with a meringue-like consistency, made with egg whites, sugar, and powdered almonds and consisting of two halves sandwiching a creamy filling

17. **MARASCHINO** *(mar-uh-SKEE-noh)* Strong, sweet liqueur made from a variety of small bitter cherries

18. **PAELLA** *(pa-EH-ya)* Spanish dish of rice, saffron, chicken, and seafood cooked and served in a large, shallow pan

19. **POKE** *(POH-kay)* Raw fish salad served as an appetizer in Hawaiian cuisine

20. **PROSCIUTTO** *(pro-ZHYOO-toe)* Italian ham cured by drying and served in very thin slices

21. **BAGUETTE** *(ba ˈget)* A long narrow loaf of French bread

22. **CROISSANT** *(k(r)wä ˈsänt, k(r)wä ˈsäN)* A French crescent-shaped roll made of sweet flaky pastry, often eaten for breakfast

23. **CRÈME BRÛLÉE** *(ˌkrem broo ˈlā)* A dessert of custard topped with caramelized sugar

24. **COQ AU VIN** *(ˌkōk ō ˈvaN, ˌkäk)* Casserole of chicken pieces cooked in red wine

25. **JIAOZI** *(jàu.tsɨ)* Chinese dumplings

26. **CHORIZO AL VINO** *(CHe ˈrēzō, -sō)* Spicy Spanish pork sausage in wine

27. **EMPANADA** *(empə ˈnädə)* Spanish or Latin American pastry turnover filled with a variety of savory ingredients and baked or fried

28. **CEVICHE** *(sə ˈvēCHā, -CHē)* South American dish of marinated raw fish or seafood, typically garnished and served as an appetizer

29. **HUEVOS RANCHEROS** *(wāvōs ran ˈCHerōs, ˌrän)* Dish of fried or poached eggs served on a tortilla with a spicy tomato sauce

30. **ARROZ CON POLLO** *(ä ˌrōs ˌkôn ˈpô(l)yô)* Spanish and Latin American dish of chicken and rice simmered with tomatoes, stock, and herbs

31. **FRIJOLES** *(frē ˈhō ˈlās)* (In Mexico) beans

32. **RAMEN** *(rämən)* Quick-cooking noodles served in a broth with meat and vegetables

33. **SASHIMI** *(sä 'SHēmē)* Japanese dish of bite-sized pieces of raw fish eaten with soy sauce and wasabi paste
34. **ANDOUILLE** *(æn'duːi/ an-DOO-ee)* Smoked sausage made using pork
35. **ÉTOUFFÉE** *or* **ETOUFFEE** *(AY-too-FAY)* Shellfish over rice
36. **SOUFFLÉ** *(so̅ofəl)* Dish made from egg yolks, beaten egg whites, and a flavoring or purée (as of seafood, fruit, or vegetables) and baked until puffed up

Foreign foods are fun! Don't get intimidated by a name any more than the flavor, texture, or taste. A person who comfortably navigates dining at a foreign restaurant shows culture and sophistication.

Let's have fun

Suggestions on ways to have fun while practicing English:

Let's go somewhere: Ask a friend to go to a foreign restaurant. Check out the menu and practice beforehand. See how well you do in pronouncing the order.

Preventing trouble

Certain situations arise when sharing food with others. Disagreements over manners, food, or paying make people look bad. Remember that such circumstances reveal character and need to be handled with tact. So, prevent trouble before it happens.

1. **REALLY WEIRD FOOD**. Pig's blood curd or deep-fried grass-hoppers may find a way to a dish in front of you. If adventurous, then try a small portion. Politely refuse if you do not wish to eat the delicacy, but refrain from insulting the host or anyone who enjoys it with comments like "Who'd eat that?" Foods can be culturally important to the host, and refusing may be considered an insult.

2. **FOREIGN SETTINGS**. Eating in the style of another culture takes study and practice. For example, eating with the Chinese by sharing food requires a different set of manners. Try to brush up on proper etiquette before eating in another culture.

3. **DIETARY CONCERNS**. Allergic reactions and dietary choices prevent people from eating certain foods. If invited to dinner, then tell the host in private when accepting the invitation about eating requirements if possible. If unable to eat food served, then don't make a scene by embarrassing the host. Just politely decline, refraining from giving the details of your medical history.

4. **DIETARY CONCERNS II**. Choosing a restaurant requires give and take. People who cannot eat certain foods and always make friends go to restaurants to suit personal needs soon find themselves at home alone due to this controlling behavior. Don't continually force personal choices on others. If the restaurant does not serve suitable food, then eat before going out or plan with the restaurant by calling ahead. Dinner is a shared experience, not just about you.

5. **BORING**. Sitting next to a boring person at a dinner party makes for a long night. A few suggestions include bringing someone else into the conversation, going to the restroom for a break, or accepting the situation by trying to enjoy it. Maybe you're just as boring!

6. **BAD ATTITUDE**. Picking the wrong restaurant makes the dinner and conversation a disappointment. Factors such as type and

quality of food, cost, location, and atmosphere create conflicts. Don't ruin dinner by bringing a bad attitude when disappointed.

7. **PAYING**. Confusion and anger can take place when sharing the bill for a large group of people. Restaurants often add an automatic tip for large parties, so the tab ends up being higher than expected. When going to a restaurant with a large group of people, decide beforehand how to pay the bill. Don't ruin a great night over a few dollars.

Question of the day

Talk about the following question with a friend or form your own opinion. Read the conversation between Emmett, Iris and Edie and then consider how you would respond. Remember to say why you think or feel as you do.

Question: What can you do when other dinner guests get angry with one another during dinner at a restaurant?

- **Emmett:** My advice is to keep quiet and stay out of the argument. If the problem has nothing to do with me then it is not my place to get involved. If they get too loud, I ask them to step outside to argue or I'll finish quickly and leave or wait outside.
- **Iris:** A friend's duty is to help resolve the issue. The first good step involves calming the combatants. If they refuse, then encouraging them to settle the issue in private to avoid embarrassment makes sense. I think that's what a friend should do.
- **Edie:** I jump right into the argument. I love it when people disagree in public. I'll often take a side. My feeling is the more people giving opinions, the faster the whole issue blows over.

What would you do in this situation? Has it happened to you in the past?

TOP TIP
PEOPLE TAKE CUSTOMS FOR EATING SERIOUSLY. A MISTAKE MAY NOT BE MENTIONED, BUT IT WILL CERTAINLY BE NOTED.

Conclusion

Conversations while eating are quite different than other types of discussions. People practice many cultural norms or family habits from who sits where, who eats first, how you eat, allowable conversation, and use of utensils. These norms impact dinner talk.

The best advice if in an unfamiliar situation is to go slow. Follow the lead of those around you and ask if confused.

Patience and practice ensures you look like a well-bred person during a dinner conversation.

Situation 7: Emotional conversations

A human being's emotions seem like a big bowl of noodles with all kinds of feelings and ideas mixed up in a big jumble. It's hard to tell where one emotion starts and one ends.

The words we use to describe our feelings in conversation can be jarring, tender, or angry.

Emotions usually deal with one of three basic human needs: love, security, or recognition, humans' most important feelings according to psychologists.

Each emotion seeks a never-ending supply of fuel to satisfy a primordial hunger not easily understood.

An individual's main job involves letting all three emotions flourish without losing control of them. The feelings compete with each other for our attention since acquiring security, love and recognition takes different skills.

In the battle for dominance sometimes-desperate inner demands cause us to blurt out words that can startle, overwhelm, hurt, or anger the world around us.

"Weakness of attitude becomes weakness of character."

Albert Einstein

Words become strident when an unsuspecting event, misfortune, or disappointment hits us. Disturbances threatening security, love, or recognition cause turmoil that unleashes pent-up, damaging words. These utterances have the ability to wreck friendships, job opportunities, or marriages.

Unacceptable behaviors wreak even more damage than passionate words. Violent or personal destructive actions need much deeper examination than this book on talking. Anyone who struggles with physical or mental explosions needs to seek professional help.

This chapter focuses on reactions such as a person's poor choice of words when attempting to deal with emotional needs.

While the other chapters in this book encourage conversation, this one urges restraint and reflection.

A crazy little thing called emotion

An emotion can pop up like an unwelcomed surprise visitor. One minute we feel great then, boom, depression, anxiety, or concern knocks on our door and barges right into our head.

Emotions fill the body from morning till night. A volatile 10-minute period in a person may go from happy, to sad, and then mad and back again. Life can be crazy!

Nobody, including the individual, knows what words may come out when dealing with those silly little things called emotions.

Emotions: Natural instinctive state of mind deriving from one's circumstances, mood, or relationships with others

Emotions shift, people change. Think about how you change in expressing yourself when happy versus sad. We've all know someone we describe as "a great person unless they get mad then watch out." The change is striking.

Let's have fun

Suggestions on ways to have fun while practicing:

- **Action activity:** Reflect on the difference between how you talk when happy, mad, and sad. Write a short paragraph describing yourself in each frame of mind and how others see you.

TOP TIP
SILENCE, A GREAT SOURCE OF STRENGTH, BECOMES VALUABLE WHEN FACING AN EMOTIONAL CRISIS.

- **Share activity:** Get together with a friend. Take turns describing each other when happy, mad, and sad. Describe how each emotion impacts you.

Different emotions, different responses

A wide range of emotions affects what we say at any one time. Let's discuss a few of life's different emotions.

Provoked: A jab to the chest

A jab in the chest provokes anger in adults, children, and animals. The response is often an unfriendly growl that says, "Stop it!

Provoke: Stimulate or incite (someone) to do or feel something, especially by arousing anger in them

To provoke means someone threatens another's love, security, or recognition, eliciting an unbecoming response. People provoke by words, intimidating actions, perceived slights, and a host of other ways.

Controlling emotions when provoked provides a challenge. A few suggestions:

1. The minute anger hits, think, "I'm upset and my judgment may be poor."
2. Some days we are sensitive. Small things easily blow up. If it's a bad day, then take a few minutes to meditate. Try to avoid volatile situations.
3. Think good thoughts. Self-doubt about love, security, or recognition causes anger. If you are provoked, relax by focusing on personal strengths.
4. Think of something funny or watch a humorous show. Humor dissipates anger.
5. Acknowledge the frustration of the situation with "So here we are"—and then jump to "How am I going to get over it?"

6. The unknown upsets us. Relax if you don't understand something. Listen carefully; be calm, quiet, and aware. Don't try too hard.

When provoked, think first then speak or act. Don't make a bad situation worse by losing control.

"Anger is an acid that can do more harm to the vessel in which it is stored than anything on to which it is poured."

Mark Twain

Anger: A lethal emotion

Anger cuts two ways. Sometimes one person gets mad. And sometimes everyone gets mad. Handling each takes a calm approach because anger is as lethal as gasoline and a match. Millions of people sit in jails around the world because when angry they set the gasoline on fire, blowing up their anger and lives.

Dealing with one's own anger depends upon an individual's personality. Some people momentarily explode then forget it while others let anger boil within only to blow up later on an unsuspecting person through an unrelated act.

Let's have fun

Suggestions on ways to have fun while practicing English:

Shared activity: Share a moment with friends about when they get angry. What causes the anger? How does it get resolved?

Let's go somewhere: Attend a city council meeting or political event to listen to angry people speak. Listen to how the speakers argue and consider whether they do a good job of expressing feelings. How could they have done a better job?

The angry conversation

Angry conversations test us. The moment of truth flashes before our eyes when we lose control of our emotions. The hardwired brain gives two basic options: fight or flight.

Fleeing only serves to heighten emotions, potentially making a bad situation worse. Hanging in and going toe-to-toe with the adversary may not be your style or cause life-altering consequences. What to do?

Running never solves much, so let's focus on the angry conversation.

Basic human instinct leads people to mimic the person steering the conversation. They scream, you scream.

An irate friend comes in yelling at you and chances are you'll be screaming right back within seconds. The risk of the friendship crumbling runs very high.

Cooler heads prevail in high-octane scenarios. Follow these suggestions when another person is angry with you.

TOP TIP
HEALTH PROFESSIONALS SAY APPROPRIATELY EXPRESSING ANGER IS HEALTHY. LETTING OTHERS KNOW AS SOON AS POSSIBLE OF DISPLEASURE RELEASES TENSION AND CLEARS THE AIR REGARDING MISUNDERSTANDINGS.

1. **GIVE THEM THE OLD ONE-TWO**: Stop the screaming by apologizing to the person for being so angry. Soothing words such as these may help:

    - "I am sorry you are so angry. That was not my intention."
    - "I'm sorry. I must have not made myself clear."
    - "I'm sorry for this disagreement."

Then find a solution by saying "Hey, let's see what we can do about this misunderstanding." Of course, a solution must be a part of the plan.

2. **APOLOGIZE IF NECESSARY**: If an apology is deserved then give a sincere one. This works if this isn't the sixth time you've said "I'm sorry" for the same offense. Also, don't apologize for something you didn't do just to calm the other person.

3. **NO BULLYING**: People create arguments to bully people into concessions. Unsavory people feed off others' unwillingness to argue to get more than they deserve. Call the person on inappropriate bullying behavior. "You said I'm stupid and that upset me. It is unacceptable. Don't do it again." If the behavior continues then the relationship needs to end.

4. **SHED LIGHT**: When being verbally attacked, shed light on the situation. Tell the truth; don't calm someone down by telling lies. Don't wait to solve the problem. Manage the problem now.

"If you are patient in one moment of anger, you will escape a hundred days of sorrow."

If a relationship does not work and cannot be fixed then so be it. That happens and life moves on. But don't end a perfectly good relationship due to harsh words in a weak moment.

Gossip: Enticing yet wrong

People love to gossip. Today's news outlets feast on the inside scoop about Hollywood stars, sports heroes, and politicians while the rest of us spread juicy tidbits about friends, fellow workers, neighbors, and schoolmates.

Gossip, an emotional conversation, spreads from teller to listener like a California wildfire. The "I shouldn't say this, but did you hear about…." conversation titillates like no other.

"Character is like a tree and reputation like a shadow. The shadow is what we think of it; the tree is the real thing."

Abraham Lincoln

But gossiping threatens all parties from the subject to the teller to the receiver. Any involvement carries the potential of damage to the reputation of others, so tread lightly because tomorrow it might be you getting hurt.

Gossip dangers

What can go wrong?

1. **GETTING PLAYED?** People tell gossip to judge your response. An unflattering response often goes straight to the talked-about person. Oops!
2. **ONCE A GOSSIP, ALWAYS A GOSSIP**: The person giving juicy tales about others loves to gossip. What makes you so special not to be a target?
3. **GOSSIP SPREADS**: No matter how much people promise, gossip spreads. If a name is attached, then count on it getting back to the talked-about individual.
4. **REPUTATION**: Spreading lies hurts reputations. People tell others gossip to spread bad news about another person, often to

their benefit. Don't count on it being truthful or nice. When you repeat it then your reputation suffers. Is it worth the damage?

Arrogance: The king's attitude

History shows numerous examples of the arrogance of kings and other rulers who believed in their magnificent power. The most arrogant despots often finished life on the end of a rope.

What have we learned from history? People rally against arrogant attitudes. Striving to show others your superiority leads people to show their dislike of you.

Obviously, arrogant attitude and speech impede communication. Condescending speech demeans listeners while creating a sense of distrust and dislike for the conceited.

Arrogance: Offensive display of superiority or self-importance; overbearing pride

Egotists need to project a superior image by degrading or humiliating others. Unfortunately, the act reflects a lack of character and strength because the need to project such an image shows a fundamental insecurity. Remember a great ego doesn't make a person great.

"It is extremely arrogant and very foolish to think that you can ever outwit your audience."

Twyla Tharp

Are you arrogant?
Check your arrogance level.
Do you:

1. **NAME DROP**. Sprinkle the names of important people you "know" in every conversation possible?
2. **AVOID EYE CONTACT**. Fail to look at the "little people" when you're talking?
3. **ARRIVE LATE**. Show up late and fail to apologize?
4. **PUT OTHERS DOWN**. Use insulting language like "That's stupid" or "Who would do that?"
5. **INTERRUPT**. Constantly interrupt others?
6. **KNOW-IT-ALL**. Always have an answer?
7. **BLAST AWAY**. Demean competitors because they can't be superior to you?
8. **PLAY THE BLAME GAME**. Always blame others for mistakes because you're never wrong?

If your conversation involves these unflattering elements, then start reining it in a bit. Trying too hard to look perfect makes you look imperfect. Don't sabotage yourself.

Blues music legend Buddy Guy wrote a song called "Your Mind's on Vacation." The song describes arrogance. See if the lyrics fit anyone you know:

Sitting there yakkin' right in my face
Coming on like you own the place
If silence was golden
You couldn't raise a dime
Cause your mind is on vacation and your mouth is working overtime

You're quoting figures, you're dropping names
You're telling stories, you're playing games
You always laugh when things ain't funny
You try to sound like you don't need money

If talk was criminal, you'd lead a life of crime
Cause your mind is on vacation and your mouth is working overtime

Ways to overcome arrogant speech

Self-important speakers unsettle others. If you struggle with arrogance then consider these tips.

1. **SEEK FEEDBACK**. Arrogance masks insecurity. Break that down by asking others for feedback or help. What are you hiding? Why are you afraid?
2. **SHARE CREDIT**. Don't accept all the credit. Share success with others, build them up, and watch things improve…success is *we*.
3. **ADMIT MISTAKES**. The arrogant wants to blame others. Own mistakes, slip-ups, and bungled opportunities…blame is *me*.
4. **BE NICE**. Superior attitudes create enemies. Friendliness speaks to concern for others while the arrogant always starts with "I…"
5. **NO I, ME, MY**. Eliminate the "me, me, me" talk from conversations.
6. **LISTEN**. Active listening makes a person focus on others, which prevents arrogant babble.
7. **OPTIMISM**. A positive approach to life aids in portraying a "we're in this together" attitude, which builds power.
8. **LITTLE**. Learn how much little will do. Arrogance makes people go overboard with self-indulgent talk. Realize that saying little produces the same results without the extra baggage of an over-inflated ego.

Love: Life's ultimate goal

The ultimate emotional conversation involves affairs of the heart, the discussion of romantic love. No other situation creates more tongue-tied, ill-conceived talking errors, omissions, and confusion than discussing personal feelings with another human being.

If the dreamy thoughts of love overcome you, then step back for a minute before diving head first into the shallow end of the pool.

Develop a strategy of how to approach this most delicate situation. Don't wait until the middle of an emotional encounter with a significant other to come up with a game plan of what to say. Plan ahead and avoid "unforced errors."

An "I love you" strategy

The 5 Ws—who, what, when, where, and why—serve as useful journalistic and talking tools. They can also give structure to a shaky foundation when discussing love.

Every important conversation needs a strategy before starting. Love conversations may be the most important conversations of all. Plan what to say before things get hot and heavy.

If you want to tell someone "I love you" then consider using the 5 Ws as a foundation:

1. **WHO**: The person receiving the emotion should be the target. Focus on the "you" not the "I" when saying "I love you." Who are they? Consider them and their feelings and interests before blurting out self-centered emotions. The talk needs to focus on them, not you.
2. **WHAT**: Consider the motivation. Telling someone "I love you" requires an examination of **what** you love about them. Those findings serve as the foundation of the conversation.
3. **WHEN**: Timing, timing, timing. When to say those magic words determines success and failure. Don't let emotions completely rule the day. Waiting for the right moment takes patience but produces powerful and long-lasting results. Make the moment special.
4. **WHERE**: Consider this in tandem with when. The location of

where to spring those fateful words plays a key role in achieving requited love.

5. **WHY**: The $64,000 question involves why. The reasons for your love need to be solid. Without a well-reasoned idea of why, "I love you" leaves the whole relationship built on lust, conquest, or confusion. Prepare for this question because the answer "I just do" doesn't cut it.

The road to love produces bumps, turns, and potholes. Well-thought-out words make the journey an enjoyable adventure.

The best advice from a yinyang perspective when facing a knee-knocking love conversation: Relax what is tense and reduce what is overflowing. Love should be a pleasing experience, not a nerve-wracking existence.

Apologizing: Owning your mistakes

The apology "Hey sorry but I'm human" doesn't hold water when telling someone you're sorry. No one would ever apologize if that made sense.

One of the most emotional conversational struggles involves the act of saying "I'm sorry" for misguided words or actions.

Admitting guilt requires figuratively bowing down in front of another and asking forgiveness. This is difficult.

But owning a mistake produces a tremendously uplifting, character-building experience. Telling another person "I'm sorry" releases guilt and provides the opportunity to reestablish a broken relationship.

The apology steps

Apologizing to a friend, family member, or acquaintance involves a several-step process.

1. **ASK FOR THE RIGHT TO APOLOGIZE**. Acknowledging the mistake doesn't mean the aggrieved will accept an apology. Ask to apologize.

2. **ADMIT YOU HURT THEM**. Once past step one, quickly admit that your words/actions hurt them. Don't equivocate by using words like "If I hurt you…" You hurt them, so admit it by saying "When I hurt you…"
3. **DISCUSS A SOLUTION**. Discuss how to improve the situation. What actions will eliminate the problem?
4. **PROMISE**. Include an assurance that the words/action will not happen again.
5. **ASK FOR FORGIVENESS**. After discussing solutions and offering a promise not to do it again, formally ask for forgiveness.
6. **SEND A NOTE**. If necessary or appropriate, consider sending a short note to follow up.
7. **GET ON WITH LIFE**. When giving or accepting an apology, let it go once done. Continually bringing up the issue means you didn't accept the apology or you're guiltier than imagined. Forgive and forget, unless, of course, the words/actions happen again.

"A stiff apology is a second insult. The injured party does not want to be compensated because he has been wronged. He wants to be healed because he has been hurt."

Gilbert K. Chesterton

Question of the day

Talk about the following question with a friend or form an opinion on your own. Read the conversation between Emmett, Iris and Edie and then consider how you would respond. Remember to explain your reasons.

Question: How do you deal with your own anger?

- **Iris:** I have a bad temper. When my mom or a friend tells me something I don't want to hear, I just lose it. I start screaming and won't stop until my anger subsides. It's just me. But when I finish, I feel good and all is usually forgotten, at least by me.
- **Emmett:** I hold my tongue while trying to figure out why I'm mad. It takes a few days to come up with a solution and those days aren't much fun. I just can't yell at another person. I don't like confrontation.
- **Edie:** I switch topics and bring up other issues that upset me. If a person blames me for something and I get angry then I'll bring up any and all things that the other person ever did to me that was wrong. It puts them on the defensive. I know it's not right but it works so who cares?

What do you think? How do you deal with anger?

Conversation: Getting angry

Snow gets angry at Sam and Spike for being late for a dinner engagement with her mother. Notice how Snow and Sunshine control their anger by using phrases such as "I think…" instead of "You should…" People respond better to "I think…" rather than "You should…" statements.

Snow: I can't <u>believe</u> Sam and Spike are late. That makes me <u>so</u> angry.

Sunshine: Now <u>calm</u> down. They'll be here soon.

Sam: Hey, girls. Sorry we're <u>late</u>.

Spike: Hello. Yeah, hope you're not <u>too</u> mad.

Snow: <u>Yes</u>, I am mad. You <u>knew</u> my mother was having dinner for us at 6 pm. We're already late and we have a 40-minute metro ride.

Sunshine: I don't <u>blame</u> Snow for being angry. I <u>think</u> you should have let us know you were going to be late.

Sam: Well Spike and I were <u>kind</u> of busy.

Spike: Yeah, we were involved in a <u>killer</u> LOL game and needed to finish.

Sunshine: You mean you two were <u>playing</u> a video game and couldn't stop?

Snow: That's <u>very</u> rude. I <u>don't</u> think you should go to dinner with us tonight.

Sam: Oh, <u>come on,</u> Snow. We're <u>sorry</u>. We just lost track of time.

Spike: Remember when <u>you</u> two never showed up for the movies because you were shopping? Mistakes <u>do</u> happen.

Snow: Well, OK. But <u>I</u> think an apology to my mother is a good idea. I'll call her now and you can apologize.

Sunshine: I think buying her a gift <u>makes</u> sense too.

Sam: OK. Let's go to the flower shop near the subway stop.

Spike: We'll <u>buy</u> her a nice bouquet of roses.

Fear, anger create emotional soup

Many emotional conversations combine fear and anger into a volatile soup. One person's fear of losing love, security, or recognition mixes with another person's anger for a dish neither wants to eat.

Let's focus on the verbal relationship between anger and fear.

1. **FEAR TO EXPRESS ANGER.** Unwillingness to express anger

can be unhealthy. Keep in mind the yinyang perspective that anger and calm involve one concept, one idea. Releasing anger often brings a person back to a healthier, calmer state of equilibrium like the push/pull door.

2. **USE "I" NOT "YOU."** Use "I" sentences when describing anger. "I feel bad when you tease me" or "I don't like it when…" Don't blame others by using "You always…" statements. Be strong by stating feelings and not blaming others. Once blaming starts, it never ends.

3. **ANGER FEEDS ON FEAR.** An angry person senses fear in others and feeds off that fear. They control that person, giving them a misguided sense of strength. The angry person continues going to the well until the fearful person builds the strength to reject the anger so it loses its power.

Conclusion

Life becomes easier when accepting the yinyang relationship of emotions. Love and hate, happiness and sadness, and anger and calm all reside in our hearts. Seek balance by not letting half an emotion control you.

Freely expressing true feelings brings peace. If others cannot accept the total you, then work needs to be done on building a more solid, honest relationship.

Situation 8:
Cross-cultural conversations

An explosion in world-wide knowledge drives today's technological and social innovation. The use of English sits at the heart of this revolution to a better future.

English attracts scientists, entrepreneurs, entertainers, political leaders, and the buying public like a magnet, exerting a pull on opportunity, growth, and progress.

The messenger for the explosion of world-wide knowledge is the Internet which allows more people than ever to share information. World citizens now consume English-based knowledge and information at breathtaking levels.

The Internet can take a local ecological innovation and make it the focus of international research, showing how the best-practices of local scientists, politicians, and citizens can improve planet Earth.

English and technology combine to build a platform for the sharing of ideas, resources, and talent, creating startling increases in the world's collective knowledge and productivity. This momentum of international education and economic opportunity is growing like Iowa corn in July and English serves as the soil providing the nutrients.

My experience at Jianghan University in Wuhan, China shows me not only the Chinese students but African and European students thirsting for English and scientific knowledge.

This accumulation and application of knowledge by the world's best and brightest people spurs innovation. The ability to speak English stands at the forefront of this innovation leap.

But even with English as a common bond, problems exist in cross-cultural communication. Cultural, political, and English-skill issues produce roadblocks that slow true dialogue.

Chances run high that during a young person's lifetime they will work, live, or negotiate with a person or people from another culture. Success comes to those best prepared to handle such communication.

Life comes fast

Columbus, Ohio's Nationwide Insurance had a popular television commercial that used the tagline "life comes at you fast."

Life does change quickly when meeting a person from another country without warning. All of a sudden, the brain strains to remember the smallest detail of a country last studied in fifth grade. They seem to know everything about your country while you mispronounce or misidentify their capital city.

Life doesn't need to be this hard. Let's break down communication problems between cultures into two categories: mental and physical.

Mentally prepared

A mentally prepared person stands ready to have a conversation with a person from any culture. An open yin side understands and accepts inevitable cultural differences but remains amenable to the experience.

A friendly person doesn't expect a foreign visitor or recent immigrant to drop all of their cultural traits and traditions whether they meet in Cleveland or Cairo. They don't lock in on preconceived notions or prejudices but stand open-minded with a smile!

Talking to a limited-English speaker

Talking to a person who speaks little English can be frustrating or fun, you decide. How you approach the conversation makes all the difference.

My advice is to keep in mind this question: "How do you think they feel?"

TOP TIP
A CRITICAL SKILL FOR YOUNG PEOPLE IN TODAY'S EVER-CHANGING WORLD INVOLVES UNDERSTANDING AND WORKING WITH OTHER CULTURES.

Points to consider when talking to a limited-English speaker:

1. **EQUALITY**. No one person is better than another. If the person struggles with English, remember that this is a second (or third!) language. Second-language speakers know the difficulty.
2. **TONE**. Be aware of the process and set a proper conversational tone. Keep the mind calm and avoid appearing frustrated. Maintain a positive and patient attitude.
3. **LIGHT**. A good speaker's touch is light, so keep the conversation moving by focusing on easy-to-understand topics.
4. **FLEXIBILITY**. Learn to see backwards, upside-down, and in-side-out. This takes time, but remaining mentally agile helps you to guess what the struggling English speaker might be saying.
5. **DEMONSTRATION.** When discussing challenging concepts, try demonstrating the idea rather than explaining it.
6. **OPENNESS.** Pay attention with an open mind free of prejudice. Cultural differences can be quite sharp. A province in China has been eating dog for thousands of years. Most other cultures don't and find it repulsive. But judging others through your own eyes doesn't always make you right and the other person wrong. It makes two different people.

Physically prepared

Physical skills come into play when communicating with a person from another culture. Be aware of the messages the body sends.

1. **EXPECT DIFFERENCES.** Handshakes, eye contact, and other ways of greeting may differ between cultures. Go slow and don't judge.
2. **RELAX AND LISTEN CAREFULLY.** Humans tense up in stressful situations, causing communication problems. Relax when not understanding and listen carefully. Be quiet, calm, and aware. Don't try too hard. Ask the person to repeat misunderstood words, but after one or two times try rephrasing the discussion or shifting the conversation topic. Realize that talking in English may not be possible.
3. **NOT VOLUME, PACE.** Speaking louder does not increase understanding, but speaking slower may help.
4. **AVOID GESTURES.** Hand gestures carry different meanings in other cultures so avoid using them.
5. **NO TOUCHING.** Many cultures do not touch a person when greeting. Don't do it unless the other person initiates the contact.

Local foreigners

Communities throughout the world become new homes to foreigners. Business and educational opportunities or the hope of a better life induce a number of people to move to a new country. Moving to China caused me problems until I got a grasp of the culture. The misunderstandings slowly slipped away as I understood cultural norms.

When moving to a new country or facing an influx of foreigners to your city prepare for an inevitable meeting by taking the time to research customs.

Jump in the water

If a foreign person or culture becomes a new part of your life, then take time to do a little work. Learning about new food, ideas and customs refreshes like jumping into a pool on a hot summer day.

When meeting a person from another culture:

1. Introduce yourself to the person. Ask about their home. Many countries have different regional customs and languages so make sure to inquire about their region.
2. Learn a few basic phrases in the language, such as hello, goodbye, how much, and numbers to start.
3. Study their customs when talking. Do they shake hands, bow, touch strangers, or make eye contact? If something confuses you then ask.
4. Go to a local public event to interact with their friends.
5. Ask to go to a local restaurant to eat food from their culture.

A powerful way to make a new friend involves taking an interest in the person's life and culture. The Chinese strongly believe in culture and truly enjoy sharing it with others. Doing business with a Chinese person usually requires cultural exchanges before discussing any business. Open your eyes by getting out of your own skin to see how others view the world.

Let's have fun

Suggestions on ways to have fun while practicing English:

- **Action activity:** Make a list of the foreign cultures in your community or region. Pick one and learn more about it.

- **Shared activity:** Learn to say hello, goodbye, and other basic phrases from another culture with a friend or relative. Practice any proper greeting gestures.

- **Let's go somewhere:** Go to a local event or restaurant to talk with people from another culture. Say hello and use the appropriate greeting manners. See if you can make a friend or two.

Question of the day

Talk about the following question with a friend or consider a view of it on your own. Read the conversation between Emmett, Iris and Edie. Then make up your own opinion. Remember to explain your reasoning.

Question: Some cultures restrict women or younger people from talking in a conversation. What do you do when two cultures' norms clash during such a conversation?

- **Iris:** I believe in the equality of the sexes no matter what. I don't believe in restricting my freedom of speech just to please another person's culture. I am going to say what I think.
- **Emmett:** I disagree, Iris. Disrespecting another person's culture to their face solves nothing while causing hard feelings between

people. Being polite and respectful makes more sense since being rude changes no one. If the person becomes your friend, then bring up differences in a more tactful way.

- **Edie:** I usually think "Is this subject worth being a jerk over?" If you get in someone's face over a cultural issue then it's like starting a war. People will defend their culture at all costs so listening stops and anger begins. You need to tread carefully.

What do you think? Do you have your own ideas?

"There are no foreign lands. It is the traveler only who is foreign."

Robert Louis Stevenson

Let's have fun

Suggestions on ways to have fun while practicing English:

- **Action activity:** Research popular entertainment in a different culture. What are favorite television shows, movies, and music?

- **Shared activity:** Find a well-known movie from another culture (dubbed or subtitled if necessary). Watch the movie with a friend or relative. After the movie, talk about what you liked or didn't like and about how the culture differs.

- **Let's go somewhere:** Go to a play, musical performance or other form of entertainment from a different culture. Learn as much as possible prior to the performance and enjoy.

On a foreign road

Visiting another country makes for exciting and confusing travel!

I know first-hand the challenge of finding restaurants, museums, and restrooms while in a Mandarin-speaking crowd. Believe me, it takes communication to another level and requires patience and ingenuity.

A few tips to help ease the process:

1. **SMILE**. Maintain a cheerful attitude regardless of the conversation's outcome. Communication may be difficult but that's not anyone's fault. Smiling always helps while panic, fear, or anger doesn't. Remember it is human nature to mimic the person talking to you. You get angry, they get angry.
2. **REMAIN CALM**. Panic sets in when lost in downtown Shanghai with 40 minutes to get to the airport. Slow down, remain calm, and look for a Starbucks. They almost always have an English speaker working on staff.
3. **CONSIDER THE LOCATION**. Many conversations involve the immediate situation or location. Focus on the surroundings. Again, demonstrate, don't explain.
4. **ASK OTHERS**. Many times, a third party who speaks both languages will be near. Ask a few people passing by for help.
5. **APP**. Foreign language apps help when visiting a foreign country or dealing with foreigners at home. Put one on your cell phone just in case. Just keep in mind they are not always accurate.

Be potent, not a punk

Modern-day attitudes about other cultures include anger, fear, and resentment. Religious, political, and economic issues pit people against each other, making true communication impossible.

Political dialogue has become increasingly limited in many countries because people with different opinions cannot even carry on simple conversations with each other without anger. Unfortunately, the angry don't realize that judgment and unrealistic demands don't solve problems.

Being open is more potent than being judgmental. Opportunities for growth open up when acknowledging others' differences. Unwillingness to recognize that others have legitimate differences makes an intolerant individual, regardless of the sanctity of the opinion.

The question becomes: Do you have to hate because others like you hate? The spread of English allows different cultures to begin to understand each other. Future progress now depends on each of us to reach out.

This book steers clear of political dogma. Let's leave this chapter on cross-cultural communication with these ideas.

Potent points

1. True goodness is being good to all. Hating, no matter the reason, invites hate into the heart.
2. Learn to unlearn. We are all taught to distrust, question, and be suspicious. Learn to unlearn habits and practices that cause us to blindly reject others who differ.
3. Accept the true knowledge of not knowing. Thinking "I know who these people are" when you only know basic differences shuts down communication. Accept not knowing.
4. Keep the heart as open as the sky. Closing the heart only brings darkness and ignorance.
5. Influence ripples out like waves on a pond. How do you want to

be known? As a closed-minded person or one who brings positive change to the world? Be aware of the emotions your words send out.

Conclusion

Foreign friends are like no others. They pull back a historical and cultural curtain of life to reveal food, ideas, and customs that you never knew existed. The view changes your life.

I've been extremely fortunate to live in China and work in a diverse institution like Jianghan University. I want to say thank you to the university and all the wonderful people from throughout the world who have taken the time to teach me about their cultures.

I've shared in other cultures thanks to spoken English. Collectively sharing the English language provides the world with a wonderful opportunity to grow together not by losing individual cultures but by sharing them.

Practice patience with the goal of using English to build a foundation of understanding and discovery between cultures. Let go of past prejudices and frozen beliefs to learn that your life isn't the only way to live.

"Make my home everywhere within the four seas. The world is my home."

TOP TIP
COMMUNICATING REQUIRES THE ABILITY TO EXCHANGE IDEAS WITH OTHERS WHO MAY DISAGREE.

Situation 9: Asking and telling

I sat holding my 12-day-old son on a cold November Sunday evening. The warmth of my newborn son gave me a feeling of peace. The phone rang and I answered it. My brother, Pat, said hello but sounded shook. "Are you sitting down?" he asked. "I have bad news."

"No. Just tell me the news," I moaned as my mind whirled about what he was about to tell me.

"Larry died in a plane crash tonight. He was one of six people who died," Pat whispered. My 24-year-old brother dead! I couldn't believe it. How could the happiest moment and saddest moment in my life be separated by only 12 days?

Asking a difficult question or telling a person life-changing information takes strength and character. My brother showed those qualities when telling me of our brother's tragic death.

Tough questions create fear of rejection. Telling bad news involves fear of the response. This chapter focuses on strength when conversations deal with tough questions and conversations.

Hard-edged questions, comments

The difficulty in asking a certain question or giving a comment depends upon circumstances. Changing dynamics and emotions make asking a question easy today but challenging tomorrow.

Certain questions or comments, however, challenge us on a consistent basis. Here are a few common examples:

Tough questions to ask others:

- Can you help me?
- Would you like to go on a date?
- Can I have a salary increase?
- Why didn't I get the promotion?
- Why did you do that?
- How come you never call me?
- What did I do wrong?

Tough things to tell people:

- No. I don't want to go.
- Sorry but your job is being terminated. I have to let you go.
- You're not who I'm looking for.
- You failed.
- I'm very angry with you.
- We need to talk about our relationship.
- Your actions upset me very much. We need to talk.

Difficult conversations come in all shapes and sizes. This chapter aims to provide a few tools to survive the challenges.

The right mind

The challenge of a difficult asking or telling situation starts in the space between your own ears. What issues do I have that make this difficult? Ask a few questions:

- Am I contemplating this action for a positive or selfish reason?

- What's the best and worst outcome if I follow through?
- Is this action necessary or are there other ways to handle the situation?

Determine your true motives prior to a confrontation. What do you stand to gain or lose in this particular situation? Understand and accept the outcome you seek, acknowledging any hidden selfishness or endgame strategy.

Get into the "right mind" by focusing on your motives and beliefs before considering the other person.

Four simple ideas should guide you:

1. **BE GENUINE**. Don't overblow the situation for impact or stretch the truth. Honestly contemplate the conversation's necessity. Get in touch with genuine feelings. No one can doubt the expression of honest feelings.

2. **RETURN TO THE LIGHT**. Difficult conversations often involve changing situations. A relationship, work, or a life situation takes a turn for the worse and needs to be discussed. Return to the positive reasons for the relationship or the situation to honestly compare and contrast the negative changes. List the changes between the new and the old. Can the positive make a comeback?

3. **BE AWARE OF IMBALANCE**. Life requires balance. The loss of balance causes relationships to fall apart and work situations to change. Determine how things became imbalanced. Where and when did expectations and results lose touch with each other?

4. **AVOID PROJECTING**. People blame others for their problems. "It's your fault!" Take ownership of your issues and don't project them onto others. Many people run from one relationship or job

to another only to find the same issues facing them. If you keep having the same tough conversations with different people then start asking yourself why you're the common denominator.

Typical weak thoughts

The need to ask a tough question makes many like a scared eight-year-old child who can't sleep in the dark.

Fear paralyzes so questions never get asked and rationalizations replace the truth. Do you say?

- "I know what they're going to say, so why ask?"
- "She never listens to me, so I'm not going to waste my time asking her again."
- "She won't say yes to me. What's the use?"
- "I just tell him what he wants, and he'll leave me alone."
- "If I just agree with her, she'll like me and hang out."

These rationalizations come out of the mouths of all people, leading to disappointing outcomes.

Yes, facing ugly or painful truths with family, friends, fellow students, teachers, and coworkers involves hurt feelings and tough conversations. Avoidance, however, delays the inevitable outcome. This allows distress to linger for days, months, or years. Life is too short to live in anguish.

At the heart of avoidance lies fear. People fear the truth so they avoid confrontations and obvious harmful situations. Today's politically correct world feeds into this dilemma by encouraging people to avoid stepping on toes. Unfortunately, it also discourages the truth.

Telling a loved one they need to lose weight or reduce drinking alcohol or smoking may upset them. But does saying nothing improve the situation if they get sick or worse?

As a young spokesperson for the Ohio Supreme Court I faced such a problem. The chief justice was going to issue an order that I thought was politically dangerous. I didn't have the nerve as a young staffer to say what I thought. When the decision blew up into a political disaster, I felt awful. I don't think saying anything would have changed the situation but I would have felt better for speaking out.

A caring person tells others the painful truth.

Asking and telling emotions

All conversations carry an emotional component. Asking and telling conversations tote an even larger share of feelings due to the sharing of sensitive or emotional information.

Let's look at three situations involving fear, overconfidence and confrontations and how they hurt communication in asking and telling.

I just can't say that

Fear causes people to refuse to ask or tell. The terror of the unknown or disagreement stops them dead in their tracks. But the dread creates more problems than the avoidance of finding out the truth.

Problems from conversational fear:

1. **FEAR CAUSES REJECTION**. Studies show confidence enhances attractiveness. The more confidence, the greater likelihood of success. People appearing afraid increase the chances of rejection,

creating a self-fulfilling prophecy. A person thinks "I am so afraid they won't pick me. I better not say anything." The picking person thinks "Oh I could never pick them. They appear so afraid that they can't talk."

2. **FEAR CAUSES MANIPULATION**. Timid people are vulnerable to manipulation by the unscrupulous seeking personal gain. Suave manipulators gain trust by keeping the fearful afraid of abandonment or dire consequences. Unfortunately, manipulators usually get what they want and leave the fearful behind anyway. Today's political and advertising worlds run on fear-based pitches.

3. **FEAR CAUSES POOR DECISIONS**. Fear creates a lack of trust. Wary individuals who don't trust make everyone untrustworthy. Examples abound of parents not trusting vaccines or doctors to help sick children, seniors not trusting banks only to be robbed, or insanely jealous people chasing away trustworthy partners.

4. **FEAR CAUSES FRUSTRATION**. Friends try to help the anxious by encouraging open and honest relations. But if deep-seated fear prevents change, then encouraging friends become frustrated trying to help the fearful person.

A speaker needs to fight through the fear to find peace.

TOP TIP
AVOIDING CONVERSATIONS INCREASES "DIS" EASE IN THE BODY THAT LEAD TO HEALTH PROBLEMS.

Overconfidence: I'm never wrong!

The flip side of fear in asking or telling is overconfidence.

Overconfidence causes people to erroneously believe that something will happen only to be proven wrong. We all do it.

Psychologists call overconfidence the most pervasive and potentially catastrophic of all the cognitive biases to which human beings fall victim. On an international level, overconfidence causes lawsuits, strikes, wars, and stock market bubbles and crashes. On a personal level, it causes divorce, lost jobs, and poor relationships.

The overconfidence effect: A well-established bias in which a person's confidence in his or her conclusion is greater than the true accuracy of the conclusions, especially when confidence is relatively high.

A speaker's overconfidence in asking or telling creates imbalance in a relationship. They believe they're correct and demand or command more than their skill, ability, or fair share deserve.

An example would be a spelling test where the respondent believes they are 100% correct when in fact they are 80% correct. A 20% error rate makes the speller look foolishly arrogant. How high is your life's error rate?

Three ways to be overconfident

A speaker looks bad when words promise big success but the action falls short of the target. They look worse when claiming success that wasn't achieved or earned.

Overconfident predictions or deceitful proclamations fill the Internet because few go back to hold prognosticators accountable. Unfortunately, real-life bosses, significant others, and friends do!

Overconfidence in telling and asking conversation includes:

1. **OVERESTIMATING ONE'S OWN PERFORMANCE**. Two problems arise when overestimating your own performance: a) Overblowing one's effort shows a lack of character by the need to "toot one's own horn," and b) Saying that you did a "great job" stops positive change. If one says they've been awesome but the situation actually needs improvement, then they're hurting not helping the situation.

2. **RANKING YOUR EFFORT HIGHER THAN OTHERS**. Saying that your efforts outperformed coworkers creates personal friction. Obviously, team efforts suffer when one claims more responsibility for success (even if it's true), causing a breakdown in morale and team building. True self-interest teaches selflessness.

3. **OVERESTIMATING**. Another overconfidence error involves the overestimation of the accuracy of one's own beliefs. Many professionals and politicians predict the future via often-inaccurate assumptions. Careers face a slippery slope when top executives' predictions prove to be inaccurate.

Successful people need vigilance regarding overconfident speech. Yesterday's success provides no guarantee that tomorrow holds the same fate, so don't cling to past success by believing "I was right today so I'll be right tomorrow." Strong leaders' words espouse humility and grace. Weak leaders' headline-grabbing predictions are usually followed up by news of a personnel shake-up at the top.

Asking and telling confrontation

Asking and telling can cause confrontations. The disagreements shake fragile people or reveal poor character in bullies.

A confrontation is defined as *a hostile or argumentative meeting or situation between opposing parties.* These situations involve work, politics, relationships, or finances.

Do you avoid confrontations? Do confrontations over asking and telling scare you?

Does this happen to you?

1. **NOT THE REAL YOU**. Worried people hide behind masks, acting in scripted ways to obscure true thoughts and feelings. People avoid work or family confrontations due to conflicting opinions with bosses or parents. Do you often find yourself saying one thing while thinking another? Do you find yourself supporting companies or people who you privately find wrong or out-of-touch with reality?

2. **ALWAYS HELPING OTHERS**. People pleasers help others while putting their own needs aside. This delays confrontations by pushing inevitable issues down the road. While appearing nice, this behavior causes resentment or burnout by refusing to deal with the truth.

3. **IT DOESN'T MATTER TO ME**. Being unassertive avoids confrontation but leads to bad health, frustration, and resentment. Pretending "I don't care" is not a short-term "solution."

4. **SAY ONE THING BUT DO ANOTHER**. Passive-aggressive people go along to avoid confrontation but often fail to follow through. They say "yes I'll do it" but end up complaining, doing a poor job, or not showing up at all.

If one of these situations describes you then decide if this is the life you want to live. How can yinyang help balance the truth with the falseness of the situation?

"I love you and, because I love you, I would sooner have you hate me for telling you the truth than adore me for telling you lies."

Pietro Aretino

Let's have fun

Suggestions on ways to have fun while practicing English:

- **Action activity:** Do you ask for help? Can you make a list of the last five times you asked for help?

- **Shared activity:** Ask a friend or relative to tell about a time when they asked for help. Share your own experiences. Talk about whether either of you like or don't like asking others for help. What are the benefits? Drawbacks?

- **Let's go somewhere:** Get together with a friend or relative. Think about something either one of you wants to buy. Prepare a list of difficult questions to ask store employees about the wanted product. Go to several stores and see what you find out.

Free to be me

The yinyang concept of freedom and captivity permeates the ability to ask and tell. Completely free people ask or tell anyone anything they please. This liberating sense of being "free to be me" gives them the opportunity to delve into all the mysteries of life while sometimes upsetting others.

The captive individual does not possess the liberty to question or honestly respond to life. The captive withholds opinions, questions, and thoughts due to a variety of reasons, creating anxiety and disappointment.

The balance between freedom and captivity is challenging. I believe the human spirit leans to the side of freedom.

Asking and telling without worry frees a person to be whole while the fearful remain muted in a personal prison. The jailer, fear, keeps people under lock and key, leaving them never to kiss the lips of sweet freedom.

Each of us owns the key to escape our personal jail, but we need to find it to open the door.

Where is the key? Behind your brain's wall of anxiety, a giant partition that supposedly protects us from the words and actions of unenlightened, uncaring, mean, or violent people.

Unfortunately, the barrier, built with half-truths, misunderstandings, a lack of confidence, denial, and an unwillingness to act, keeps us hidden but unfulfilled. The risk of obtaining freedom involves facing rejection, confrontation, and failure. This high price forces many to keep quiet, subservient, and miserable.

Freedom requires building speaking strength. Talking confidence allows the real you to emerge, the wonderful individual behind the barricade. Truth is like a caged animal that wants to escape and run free.

"He who sees through all fear will always be safe."

Free to be unafraid

Fear: An emotional response to a perceived threat.

Fear exists in us all. Our hardwired brains spot danger, sending the message to fight or flee the fear-inducing menace. If fear of speaking always makes you flee then keep these thoughts in mind.

1. **BE PRESENT**. Yesterday and tomorrow are illusions in life. Live freely in the present moment and don't let what *could* happen stop you from what *is* happening.

2. **LET THE FANTASY GO.** People love to live in a fantasy world where all turns out brilliantly in the end by keeping their mouth shut. Maybe you'll be one that beats the long odds in this fantasy world, but don't bet on it. Let go and live today.

3. **FEAR IS AN ILLUSION**. Fear stops us from enjoying life. How many times do you say "That looks fun but I could never do it?" Overcoming fear liberates. If talking creates fear then start small. Start the journey with one or two words where once there were none.

4. **CHANGE**. The fear of change inhibits us all, but all things change. Short-sighted efforts keep us quiet until inevitable change comes. Provide input; don't stay quiet waiting for change.

5. **WATER IS SOFT**. The quote "water is soft but overcomes the hard" needs to be a part of the mantra of a quiet or shy person. Soft word can achieve results. A kind spirit changes the world by being true to their character and letting others know how they feel in a genuine yet soft voice.

You are true and false

Yinyang accepts true and false as one. It can't be anything else. Life is a balance between true and false.

Life improves the closer we live in truth. When the authentic person rises like a bright summer sun, beautiful things happen. It's called personal acceptance.

Many religious dogmas preach the words "the truth shall set you free." Here are a few reasons how:

1. **FEWER WORRIES**. Honesty reduces worries. No more need to hide.
2. **EMPOWERMENT**. The truth gives a sense of power to all who touch it.
3. **RESPECT**. Truth brings respect.
4. **PEACE**. Living a lie causes anxiety, stress, anger, and depression. Freedom brings peace.
5. **DISCOVERY**. Truth brings out the real you. Life is too short not to be authentic.

11 freedom tips

If you want to be "free to be me" then a price needs to be paid. The cost involves the willingness to let others know what you want, need, or think.

This is hard to do. Preparing to tell another person bad or upsetting news or asking a difficult question requires careful thought, planning, and strength. Going in with a plan makes the task easier.

1. **PREPARE AN OUTLINE**. Write a script and practice it.
2. **GET TO THE POINT**. Keep small talk to a minimum. Avoid rambling on about unimportant details that confuse the listener.
3. **PICK THE RIGHT SETTING**. Location is important. Pick a comfortable and safe location if possible.
4. **PICK AN APPROPRIATE TIME**. Don't unload on someone who just finished a busy day. Decide on a time that allows for enough opportunity to fully discuss the matter.
5. **SIGNAL THE COMING BAD NEWS OR HARD QUESTIONS**. A beginning phrase such as "I need to talk to you" or "Something has been bothering me that I want to discuss" sets the right tone.
6. **TOO MUCH**. Emotional or difficult conversations have the potential to get out of hand. Using too much force when telling someone bad news can backfire. Stay composed, only being harsh or forceful when necessary.
7. **OFFER COMFORT**. If the news causes anguish or pain, consider offering comfort following the conversation. This may or may not be appropriate.
8. **NO RESPONSE**. The other person may not respond to comments or questions because they need time to process the information. If they say nothing, then don't force them. Thank them for their time and let them know the importance of the matter. If necessary, express a willingness to further discuss the matter.
9. **TOO MUCH RESPONSE**. Anger or hostility may be an outcome of a difficult discussion. If concerned about violence towards you then bring a friend or hold the discussion in a public location.
10. **PROFESSIONAL HELP**. Working through difficult situations may require professional help. Qualified professionals such as psychologists, mediators, and attorneys assist disagreeing parties.
11. **WHAT'S NEXT?** After the discussion, consider how the

conversation unfolded and determine the next move. A second or third discussion may be necessary before resolution.

Question of the day

Talk about the following question with a friend or form an opinion on your own. Read the conversation between Emmett, Iris and Edie and then consider how you would respond. Remember to explain your reasoning.

Question: Do you find it easy asking for help?

- **Iris:** I have no problem asking another person for help. Most people want to help you, especially friends or family. Why feel embarrassed? The time saved or worry solved far outweighs concerns over asking.
- **Emmett:** No. Asking for help is simply a sign of weakness. I have no interest in sharing my ignorance or concerns with friends or strangers. I think I'm smart enough to figure things out on my own with the help of the Internet.
- **Edie:** It depends on the situation. If I'm lost and need directions, then asking a local to point me the right way makes sense. If I have a personal problem, then I'm more likely to seek the help of a professional than to ask a friend or family member. I accept I don't know everything, but sharing with friends leads to gossip.

What do you think? Do you ask for help?

Conversation

Snow is the director of the school play, *To Kill a Mockingbird*. Spike tried out for the lead character, Atticus Finch. He wants to ask Snow if he got the part, and she needs to tell him that he did not.

Spike: Hey, Snow. I know you are going to post the parts for the play tomorrow. I was wondering if you can let me know *now*? I am *so* nervous that sleeping would be *impossible* tonight.

Snow: Sure, Spike. Let's sit down and *talk* about it.

Spike: Oh-oh. *That* doesn't sound promising. *(He laughs nervously.)*

Snow: I *really* appreciate how much effort you put into the try-outs Spike. You clearly have acting talent, and I want to help you.

Spike: I did my *best* by reading the novel, watching the movie, and studying all the lines. I *was* prepared.

Snow: *That's* obvious. But, *unfortunately*, I am going to cast Sam as the lead. Let me explain *why*. Atticus Finch is a tall man who is soft-spoken but strong. The character *requires* these traits. Sam *fits* these requirements. Before you get *too* upset I have something to ask you. Would you be interested in playing *Boo Radley*, a very important character in the play as well? I believe you would be *excellent*.

Spike: I *did* want to play the lead, but I wondered as well if I was right for the part. I also thought Boo Radley *might* be a better fit for me.

Snow: We *need* your dedication and knowledge of the play for it to be a success. Will you *do it* with us?

Spike: Sure. You can count on me. I can help Sam with his part as well. I know <u>all</u> of Atticus' lines.

Snow: Thank you for understanding, Spike. If we all work together, we can make this a great production.

Surprise reactions

Tough conversations have real consequences. Serious talks threaten safety, feelings, families, money, pride, love, or respect, creating unpredictable and surprising reactions.

Facing the facts of a situation takes strength, and handling it takes character. Do you have what it takes?

Bad news responses

A variety of responses occur when giving bad news. Here are a few:

1. **ANGER**. People get angry when hearing bad news. Carefully plan a discussion when the potential of anger exists. Public locations can keep situations under control. Also choose a time when the other person is less likely to be agitated, such as early in the day. Avoid situations where alcohol is involved.
2. **TEARS**. Tough conversations evoke tears, so remain steadfast in a conviction. Melting due to tears makes someone disappointed …you. No one wants to see another cry, but if the reasons make sense then show resolve.
3. **REVENGE**. Forcing a situation may get the right results, but

people can get upset and plot revenge. They may feel motivated to "pay you back." Keep your wits if threatened. Try to calm the other person, but make sure not to leave yourself vulnerable.

4. **DENIAL.** Some individuals simply do not believe bad news. They act as if you didn't mean it or try to win favor back through acts of kindness. Again, these situations require a kind but firm response.

Let's have fun

Suggestions on ways to have fun while practicing English:

- **Action activity:** Think about something you need to tell or ask someone. Draw up a plan for when, where, and what you should say.

- **Shared activity:** Talk to a friend or relative about something they want or need to ask. Tell each other your plans and discuss why it is hard to follow through.

- **Let's go somewhere:** Go to a local small claims court and listen to the judge and defendants discuss legal cases. Listen to the way they ask and tell each other things. If you get a chance, ask a judge or attorney what they do when asking or telling difficult points in court.

Conclusion

Nothing tests a human's resolve more than asking a tough question or telling bad news. I wrote this book because of my lifetime of struggles with these two bedeviling topics.

To get past doubt, people must answer tough personal questions like:

- Am I weak or just considerate?
- Do I have what it takes to do what's right?
- Do I really want something so much that it causes pain in others?
- How much more can I take?

These questions often get to the heart of whether we say something or keep quiet. They decide if we really want to be "free to be me."

"He who asks is a fool for five minutes, but he who does not ask remains a fool forever."

Situation 10: Talking's dark side

The yinyang of white and black carries many shades of grey. A cold, dingy grey winter sky and a warm, comforting grey bedroom create different emotions within the black and white dynamic.

The dark and light side of talking involves a similar range of textures, feelings, and emotions. The dark brings brooding, angry words, stopping conversations, instilling fear, and chilling the air. The light brings bright, comforting words, stimulating conversation, exciting people, and encouraging life and growth.

The stream of life gives us the opportunity to use a wide range of dark and light words in conversation. This chapter focuses on the dark side of conversations that reflect poorly on a speaker and hinder communication.

Humans live on both the sunny and dark side of the mountain when speaking English.

Talking's eight deadly sins

Great conversation involves confident, strong people who enjoy the give and take of open, honest discussion. Anything that impedes the free flow of conversation serves as a roadblock to the outcome.

Conversation's eight deadly sins show where common talking missteps hinder the flow of communication. We all commit these sins from time to time so be on guard for when they pop up in your speech.

Conversation's eight deadly sins:

1. **TALKING ABOUT OTHERS**. Everybody gossips. People like to talk about other people. However, when gossiping becomes a focal point of all conversations then people soon see the gossiper as a mean, petty person. Remember the saying, "If you have nothing nice to say, then say nothing at all." Limit gossiping.

2. **NEGATIVITY.** A negative person makes the world seem like a horror movie filled with monsters and demons who want to ruin life. Continual distressing talk becomes depressing and drives people away. Balance the good with the bad.

3. **JUDGMENT.** Harsh judgment of others makes people appear cruel. Criticizing people's clothes, hair, race, religion, looks, intelligence, decisions, finances, or weight creates ill will. Set the right tone.

4. **WAH-WAH-WAH**. Nobody likes a complainer. Sure, an individual should share valuable information about poor service or a cheat, but constantly whining gets old. Once the blaming and complaining starts, it never ends. Limit complaining. Everyone faces problems.

5. **MY ALARM CLOCK BROKE**. Losers make excuses. Repeated excuses to friends or bosses for bad behavior reveal a person failing to live up to their word. This behavior chases friends and jobs away. Excuses are the words of losers.

6. **DISHONESTY.** Excuses are bad, lying is worse. No one likes a liar, especially friends, family, and coworkers.

7. **LET ME TELL YOU.** People who "know everything" monopolize conversations and eventually lose credibility. No one knows everything but that doesn't stop the know-it-all. Dubious answers, pointless facts, and constant talking block the two-way street of communication. People needing to show intelligence usually aren't that smart.

8. **WAIT...BEFORE YOU GO ON.** The interrupter stops every conversation because they never let anyone finish a sentence. Interrupters are inconsiderate. Keep your mouth shut when someone else has the floor. Conversation isn't a competition to see who talks the most.

TOP TIP
MASTERING OTHERS IS STRENGTH, MASTERING YOURSELF IS TRUE POWER.

Distractions

Good conversationalists make it easy for the listener to hear and understand the message. Positive speaking techniques such as clear diction, hand gestures, facial expressions, and emphasis encourage the free flow of information.

Negative speech habits do the opposite, distracting listeners and causing communication breakdowns. Distractions annoy a listener like a late-night mosquito buzzing around a sleeper's head.

Talking tics (distracting words and motions), improper volume, excessive profane or technical terms, and cellphones set up barriers to communication success. Avoid them. Here are a few examples:

1. **AH-AH-AH**. The dreaded ahhhhhs, ummmms, mmmms, and wellllls hurt the flow of words and thought. Effective interjections help to punctuate or build conversation to a point. Too many ahhhs in a sentence makes a speaker appear unprepared, unskilled, untrustworthy, or unintelligent. Silence, a great source of strength, provides a better alternative.

2. **REPEATING CATCHWORDS**. The repeated use of the word "like" became a 1980s American craze. Started by teenagers (valley girls) from Southern California who used sentences such as "Like I was going to the mall and like I saw this bitchin' guy who like looked at me…" This way of speaking lives on today. Words such as *awesome, nice, that makes sense, I see, really, dude,* and *sure* replaced like. We are creatures of habit who get stuck using the same phrase over and over within the same conversation. The continual use distracts listeners and reflects poorly on the speaker. Mix it up by avoiding the same word or phrase over and over in speaking or writing.

3. **CONVERSATION HOGS**. Some people don't know when to shut up. They monopolize a conversation, barely breathing so as not to give anyone else a chance to talk. Listening, asking questions, and letting others talk encourages a two-way conversation. Don't monopolize conversations.

4. **MUMBLERS AND WHISPERERS**. Speakers control conversations by volume and clarity. Mumblers and whisperers make listeners struggle to hear or understand conversations. Be kind to listeners by speaking as clearly and loudly as necessary.

5. **PROFANE LANGUAGE**. Today's verbal craze is cussing. Users expect shock by repeated f-bombs but come across as lame as a valley girl who uses "like" all the time. A properly used, occasional cussword is an effective language tool. Overuse casts a

poor light on a speaker just as repeatedly using the same adjective. Also, avoid inappropriate language in front of children or in professional settings. When in doubt, keep it clean.

6. **TECHNICAL, POLITICAL, OR DIVISIVE WORDS.** Much like swearing, technical, political, and highly charged topics don't have a place in every conversation. Polite conversationalists know when not to talk above an audience, rant about political beliefs, or share fervent religious views. Know the audience.

7. **CELLPHONE CONVERSATIONS.** Cellphones don't mix with conversation. Two main points: a.) Avoid the cellphone during conversation. Using the phone says to a guest, "You're not that important." Do you want to hear that? Answer only absolutely necessary calls or texts, and b.) Don't force others to listen to personal calls. Friends or strangers don't care about your life, what you're having for dinner, or your opinion of the new Netflix series.

Question of the day

Talk about the following question with a friend or form an opinion on your own. Read the conversation between Emmett, Iris and Edie and then consider how you would respond. Remember to explain your reasoning.

Question: Which of the eight deadly talking sins bothers you the most?

- **Emmett:** People who think they know everything drive me crazy. Conversations turn into an excuse for them to go on and on about how much they know. They rarely listen, always interrupting. I want to choke them.

- **Iris:** I agree, know-it-alls are difficult. But for me, complainers take the cake. They constantly moan and groan. The food stinks. The weather's awful. Their friend is mean. They feel bad. I want to scream, "Please stop complaining!"
- **Edie:** People who constantly interrupt others are the rudest people alive. They believe what they say is more important or smarter than anyone's comments. I don't see what's so hard about letting a person finish before butting into a conversation.

What do you think? Which deadly talking sin bothers you?

"Watch out for the joy-stealers: gossip, criticism, complaining, faultfinding and a negative, judgmental attitude."

Joyce Meyer

Let's have fun

Suggestions on ways to have fun while practicing English:

- **Action activity:** Look at talking's eight deadly sins. Which sins do you commit? Are you guilty with everyone or just certain people who bring out the worst in you?

- **Shared activity:** Have a conversation about the deadly sins with a friend or relative. Talk about why people commit the sins, which ones you commit the most, and what a person can do to stop "sinning."

- **Let's go somewhere:** Go to a party or dinner. Listen to conversations and make mental notes of the most popular deadly sins used. Watch how listeners respond.

Conversation

Snow, Sunshine, Sam, and Spike go out to lunch. Listen to how using the eight deadly sins in conversation affects the interaction between them.

Snow: I hope you guys _like_ this restaurant. Casa Mexico has _great_ Mexican food.

Spike: I _hate_ Mexican food. It's all just beans and _rice_. I don't know _why_ I came.

Snow: Welllll... _You_ picked the last restaurant, Spike, and hmmmmmm it was awful. I thought, well maybe, we could ahhhhhh go someplace hmmmmm new.

Sam: Yeah, Spike. _Cool_ it. You're always _whining_. It really becomes _old_ after a while.

Spike: Ahhh. Snow goes to places she knows _I_ won't like.

Snow: _That's_ not true, Spike. It's not my fault that _all_ you eat are hamburgers and French fries. You have no...

Sunshine: This is the _best_ restaurant in town according to our-town.com. If I were _you,_ I'd order the number 3 special with extra sauce. If you order anything else, you are _clueless_.

Snow: What? I was _saying_ that Spike...

Sunshine: The _desserts_ are wonderful. And healthy. They only use _natural_ ingredients and everybody knows that is the best way to go. I _never_ eat any trans-fats. Totally bad, bad, bad. If you guys would just _listen_ to me your lives would be so much better.

Sam: What made _you_ so smart, Sunshine? You act…

Sunshine: I _do_ know more than you, Sam.

Sam: Let me finish a sentence. You…

Sunshine: _Please,_ Sam. No one wants to hear what _you_ have to say. You're just a _big dumb jock_.

"Show class, have pride and display character. If you do then winning takes care of itself."

Paul Byrant

Warning signs

The dark side of talking ensnares even the best English speakers. Inserting thoughtless or careless words into conversation threatens careers, relationships, and family harmony.

If not vigilant, then it becomes easy to fall prey to the allure of gossip, complaining, ego-driven comments, or negativity.

Dangerous verbal lubricants include false encouragement from others, alcohol, and the promise of reward. Don't become the victim!

Feeling the urge to go to conversation's dark side? Let these tips keep you strong.

1. **GROWTH.** Too many times people interrupt conversations so they can talk about their "reputation" as if it is a frozen relic of the past. The old standard "Well I always…" kills conversation. Growth requires change not clinging to the past. Stop telling your same old stories that no one wants to hear again.

2. **CLARITY...CLARITY...CLARITY.** Don't obscure a message by using technical jargon, cusswords, poor volume, or talking tics. Make sure the words hit the intended target with clarity. Less is more.

3. **WHAT ABOUT YOU?** The unchecked ego brings rigidity and death to a conversation. The act of caring about others brings life and growth. Don't let the "know-it-all" ego strangle the life out of a conversation.

4. **SECURITY.** Preparing for a difficult conversation by loading up with all sorts of ammunition? The more weapons means the less secure you feel. Too much firepower reveals insecurity. Stick to several simple, well-thought-out points rather than overwhelming listeners with jargon, confusing theories, and bluster.

5. **LEAVE ROOM IN THE BOWL.** Filling a bowl of soup to the brim causes it to spill. Conversations filled to the brim lose effectiveness. Don't overwhelm listeners with too much talking. Brains can't consume that much information, leaving much of the effort wasted. Intrigue people by leaving them wanting more.

6. **STAY GROUNDED.** People imitate other talkers. He gossips, I gossip. She complains, I complain. The allure of gossip and negativity entraps people into saying harmful things. When this happens, ask "Must I value what others value?" Be grounded by knowing who you are and what's important. Don't get sucked into negative conversations that reflect poorly on you.

Be always vigilant to the dark side of conversation. Stay strong and remember that mastering others is strength but mastering yourself is true power.

CONCLUSION

Communication shouldn't be a game of hide and seek where the speaker conceals the message among unnecessary words or physical acts. Excellent English speakers seek clarity and balance.

The dark side of conversation clouds communication by focusing on negative comments, irrelevant points, and distracting words or actions.

Keep things clear by removing the barriers. This requires an occasional scan of your speaking. Are you using certain phrases too often? Using your cellphone excessively? Swearing too much?

Clean up conversation patterns and habits from time to time so your messages continue to get through.

"I'd rather die for speaking out, than to live and be silent."

TALKING STRATEGIES

ACHIEVING LIFE GOALS

A talking game plan

THIS BOOK STRESSES THE IMPORTANCE of mindfulness when talking. The idea is simple, if you pay attention to what you say then better things happen.

Casual conversations with friends and family allow one to relax so less attention gets paid to the words that come out. Nothing much will change in the relationship if there is a verbal slip-up.

But other situations involving work, interviews, tests, and life-changing discussions require intense mindfulness. Every word matters.

This chapter focuses on the times when we must pay close attention to what we say.

It's more than just talk

Conversations' value, meaning, or importance change depending upon the situation.

How much attention do you pay when discussing the following situations?

- A conversation about the sudden death of a friend
- Your favorite flavor of ice cream with a young child
- A job interview with the president of a company

Hopefully these situations create different levels of thought and attention!

A second question then follows: Do you spend the same amount of time preparing for each conversation? The answer should be, "Of course not." The importance determines the amount of preparation.

Important conversations need strategies that involve thought and plans. Here are six steps in preparing for an important conversation:

1. **WHAT'S THE CONVERSATION?** What will be discussed and why is it important to you? Is it important to the other person?

2. **WHERE DO YOU STAND?** What is your position and authority in the conversation? Are you an expert? Employee? Concerned friend? In developing a strategy accept your position and develop a plan befitting that position.

3. **IDENTIFY WHAT'S IMPORTANT?** What do you want to accomplish in the conversation? In developing a strategy set goals and fallback positions. You may WANT this but you'll ACCEPT that.

4. **KNOW THE AUDIENCE.** Who are you talking to and how will they respond? Try to imagine how the other person or people will think and react. Use your intelligence of them to consider strategies.

5. **PREPARE AND REVIEW.** Develop 2-4 key points spelling out thoughts and ideas. Why do your comments make sense? How will they improve the situation? It's better to have a few well-prepared points than a laundry list of demands.

6. **FLEXIBLE?** Determine your flexibility during the conversation. Will you be open-minded and nimble if things shift or will you remain steadfast in your ideas or requests?

Types of talk

People decide what to say using four basic methods: Instinct, habit, emotion, and strategy. Each method has advantages and disadvantages. Let's take a brief look at each method:

1. **INSTINCT:** An innate, typically fixed pattern of behavior in animals in response to certain stimuli. Words from deep within are often termed "guttural." You smack your finger with a hammer, you say "ouch." Something happens to you and inner forces take over and respond. Much of language comes from our animal instincts.

2. **HABIT:** A settled or regular tendency or practice, especially one that is hard to give up. A habit when passing a friend on the street may be saying "hello" with a nod or wave while continuing on our way. Conversation patterns are made up of countless phrases repeated over and over.

3. **EMOTIONAL:** Arousing or characterized by intense feeling. The emotional human speaks with a stream of passionate words revealing inner feelings. Anger, love, excitement, and depression all come out in a flurry of words and actions. These emotional outbursts may be habitual, instinctual, or a rare occurrence.

4. **STRATEGY:** A plan of action or policy designed to achieve a major or overall aim. A speaking strategy is used when attempting to accomplish a specific goal. A methodical plan seeks to achieve goals where instincts, habits, and emotions fail. The strategy can be complex or simple as smiling and saying "hello" to an important person you want to meet.

While most conversations involve the first three methods, this chapter focuses on the critical ability to incorporate strategy into conversations.

Accomplishing a life goal

We all have things in life we want. Maybe a good job or a romantic relationship tops your list. What can you do to achieve success? Well, I believe, success finds those with excellent skills.

Let's start with the basics:

Style

The first step in developing a strategy to achieve a goal starts with a phrase we introduced earlier in the book: "What's in your refrigerator?"

An English speaker develops excellence by identifying strong and weak skills. No coach ever goes into a game without knowing both teams' strengths and weaknesses. If accomplishing a goal involves speaking English then examine your skills and determine where your excellence lies. What's in your speaking "refrigerator?"

This refers to talking style, your physical and aural traits. Are you a soft-spoken intellectual who uses a minimal amount of physical gestures or a gregarious fellow who pats backs, tells jokes, and laughs out loud?

Trying to be something you're not guarantees serious problems. Too many times people face an important meeting by forgetting who they are. That strategy is wrong. Don't hide who you are but find ways to make yourself strong as possible.

Talking style is a tough habit to change. People rarely change talking style after the age of three years old because style and personality are so closely linked.

Any talking style works as long as it's authentic. Accept who you are and be the best you can be. A person trying to be someone they're not is as out of place as a bald man at the barbershop.

Style doesn't prevent one from accomplishing a goal. All styles work as long as presented in the best possible light. Section Six goes into greater detail on improving talking style.

Strategy

The second step in attaining a goal involves incorporating a plan that combines talking style with sound strategy.

While a person's style remains consistent, strategy changes depending upon the shifting goals of life.

Consider using style and strategy like a basketball team. The team's style rarely changes during a basketball season. A team may have short but very fast players so it competes at a lightning pace instead of slow or physical.

If the team plays a big, slow team then they use pressure and run all the time. When playing a short but even faster team then they slow the pace and focus on defense.

The goal for every speaker involves putting together a style and strategy that meshes into a winning personal communication formula for that situation.

TOP TIP
A SPEAKER CHANGES STRATEGY LIKE A COACH CALLS PLAYS BASED ON ADVANTAGES OVER AN OPPONENT.

The talking strategy

Saying the right thing is the goal for any speaker. But what is the right thing to say?

This book recommends a thoughtful, patient approach when talking. People consider polite speakers strong in character because they generally seek cooperation rather than conflict. But does that make them pushovers? Many believe the old saying, "Nice guys finish last."

Today's media celebrate rude and combative comments. Many famous people build an Internet following on the ability to create attention by outrageous headline-grabbing comments.

The Internet encourages ordinary people to follow this approach by allowing them to hide behind anonymous screen names while spewing insults and wild comments as if they're 12th century invaders throwing rocks over a wall into a crowd.

That aggressive style works for the nameless Internet scribe but not when talking to a boss, friend, or family member or using your real name when posting divisive comments. Stories fill news feeds regarding people losing jobs for inappropriate spoken or written comments.

Bashing, complimenting, or questioning people's opinions, ideas, politics, skin color, religion, or gender under an assumed Internet name involves no personal courage or intelligence.

TOP TIP
PUBLIC COMMENTS REQUIRE TACT AND STRATEGY.

A sound speaking strategy provides a plan of action to defend, explain, and promote opinions, thoughts, and ideas in face-to-face conversations where others examine ideas and respond in kind. A solid talking plan involves character, confidence, strength, and risk.

Conflicting interests

Many conversations involve differing interests between speakers. A well-designed strategy seeks to solve the problem of conflicting interests in the least confrontational way possible.

Let's look at two common conflicts of interest in conversation.

The first conflict deals with the individual's balance of self-interest with relationship building.

A typical speaking issue: I want to "win" the conversation with my boss but at what cost? Will my "opponent" (the boss) love, like, or respect me when done? How do I get what I want without upsetting the boss and getting fired? All are difficult to answer.

Success means little if it requires verbally stomping on your boss to get it and paying a heavy price like losing your job for "victory." But on the other hand, who wants to be a total "yes" person who never disagrees? We all want our own definition of success and respect.

Solid strategy allows a speaker to achieve a goal and maintain support.

The second conflict examines the idea of a "win-win" agreement. How can we both succeed? I want something and my boss or girlfriend wants something else. I want attention; my boss wants production. I want love; my girlfriend wants security. I want money; my boss wants more money. How can I facilitate an agreement where both parties feel satisfied?

Solid strategy can also achieve a "win-win" scenario.

Convincing others

How many ways exist to convince another person to "give in" when facing a conflict of interest? Too many to count is the answer.

People use kind words, threats, guilt, and flattery to name a few. Some consider relationship building or support as important while others just care about winning and will do what it takes.

Fourteen common ways to convince:

1. The promise of something positive in return
2. The promise of something negative in return
3. Flattery
4. Threats
5. Anger/bullying/badgering
6. Logic
7. Guilt
8. Allure
9. Consensus
10. It's the right thing to do
11. Expediency
12. Humor
13. Lies
14. Combination of several of these ways.

The number of ways to convince explodes when adding how people use body language, eye contact, touch, talking speed, tone, and other psychological or emotional tricks to the 14 common ways to convince.

So what is the best way to get what you want?

Science points in a certain direction when finding an answer to this perplexing question.

Game theory:
A Nobel Prize-winning strategy

Negotiating conflicts of interest boils down to something like horse trading. For example, instead of saying, "I'll give you the white horse for the brown one" we say "I'll give you money if you give me 40 hours of work each week." Both parties must decide if the trade is fair.

The "transactions" become very tough-minded when threats come into play such as, "You'll give me money or I'll see you in court" or "You do what I say or you're fired!"

People face a wide array of potential communication situations. Can people follow one strategy that helps answer most "transactional" conversations involving conflicts of interests? The study of game theory provides an answer.

Game theory analyzes situations involving conflicting interests (as in business or military strategy) in terms of gains and losses among opposing players. Nine Nobel Prizes have been awarded to scientists studying this topic.

Let's take a look at game theory as a useful talking strategy.

"If you don't know where you're going, any road will get you there."

Lewis Carroll

The prisoner's dilemma game

Game theory came from scientists' search for the best way to solve conflicts of interest.

Two researchers, Merrill M. Flood and Melvin Dresher, invented the Prisoner's Dilemma game in 1950 to examine a baffling conflict of interest scenario.

Here's the premise:

The police arrest you and an associate. The two of you were smart and shredded the evidence but each face a year in prison. But the prosecutor wants to nail someone, so he offers a deal: by squealing on your associate — which results in a five-year jail sentence for him — the prosecutor will take six months off your sentence. This sounds good, until you realize the prosecutor is offering the same deal to your associate— which gets you a five-year stretch.

So what to do? The best plan is to agree to not squeal but cooperate in a mutual bond of silence, and do a year in jail.

But wait: if your associate goes along with silence, should you squeal (defect) and get that six-month reduction?

It's tempting, but then he's also tempted. And if you both squeal, oh, no, it's four and a half years each.

Perhaps cooperating makes sense — but wait, that's being a sucker, as your associate will surely defect, and you won't even get the six months off. So what is the best strategy to minimize your incarceration?

Do you squeal on your associate or not? This simple question (and the implicit question of whether to trust or not), expresses a crucial issue across a broad range of life questions and talking situations.

The game's dilemma highlights daily struggles of deciding who to support, trust, or follow. Do we try to convince to benefit ourselves to the detriment of another individual or the rest of society, or do we support the group or community to the detriment of ourselves? How do we convince? What is the best strategy to take?

The best approach

Political scientist Robert Axelrod set out to determine the best approach in the Prisoner's Dilemma.

Axelrod solicited game theorists to compete in a Prisoner's Dilemma tournament. The tournament's goal was to determine the best strategy in conflicting situations.

Strategies included always looking out for your own best interests, always deferring to the other person, and all strategies in between.

Each strategy was paired with the other strategies for 200 iterations of a Prisoner's Dilemma game. Axelrod kept score on the total points accumulated through the tournament.

A strategy called "TIT FOR TAT" (TFT) won. The strategy involves cooperating on the first move and then echoing what the other player does on every subsequent move.

The results of the tournament were analyzed and published, and a second tournament was held to see if anyone could find a better strategy. TIT FOR TAT won again.

Axelrod analyzed the results and made interesting discoveries about the nature of cooperation, which he describes in his book *The Evolution of Cooperation*.

Four main points

Axelrod's book revealed four major conclusions involving game strategy.

1. **BE NICE:** Never be the one to defect first. Many competitors went to great lengths to gain an advantage over the "nice" (and usually simpler) strategies, but to no avail: tricky strategies, fighting for a few points, generally failed compared to nice strategies. TFT (and other "nice" strategies) "won, not by doing better than the other player, but by eliciting cooperation [and] by promoting the mutual interest rather than by exploiting the other's weakness."

2. **BE WILLING TO RESPOND:** Being nice all the time also leads to being used, suckered, or taken advantage of in situations. Axelrod's study shows the necessity to respond in a like manner, nice for nice and defection for defection. The key is to return to cooperation as soon as the other person does. Overdoing punishment causes negative escalation in the relationship and a never-ending series of defections, which leads to failure.

3. **DON'T BE ENVIOUS:** This strategy concedes that you will be no better off than the other person. This "good as the other person" strategy allowed TIT FOR TAT to always come in tied for first place regardless of the other strategy. Axelrod saw this as the ability of the person not to be envious but to accept the cooperative nature of the relationship.

4. **DON'T BE TOO TRICKY:** Being too clever causes confusion. Clarity is essential for others to cooperate with you. Hiding or secretly manipulating leads to defections.

The four suggestions provide a speaker the ability to consistently "win" while building community and should be the heart of a talking strategy.

It requires willingness to:

- Cooperate at the beginning and be nice. Be aware of the process. The leader's stability sets the tone.
- Have the strength to respond in kind. Defect when they defect and cooperate when they cooperate. A leader learns to follow.
- Accept the other's success when cooperating. True self-interest teaches selflessness.
- Trust and be trustworthy. Don't try to outfox them. Not trusting people makes you untrustworthy.

Question of the day

Talk about the following question with a friend or form an opinion on your own. Read the conversation between Emmett, Iris and Edie and then consider how you would respond. Remember to explain your reasoning.

Question: Do you use a talking strategy?

- **Emmett:** No, I can't say that I do. My only "strategy" is to keep light on my feet and dance around any complicated issues that arise in a conversation. My feeling is you don't know where the conversation will go so just remain ready.
- **Iris:** I always prepare a strategy when facing a difficult situation. I consider what a successful outcome is then work on getting it. This allows me to consider a fallback position when needing to negotiate a settlement.
- **Edie:** I have one strategy: Come in blasting away and the last person standing wins. I know what I want and won't settle for second place. I realize the strategy upsets many people but I was born to win.

Which way do you feel is the most effective way to negotiate?

Conclusion

A talking strategy should be a part of any winning conversation. If you don't take the time to plan then the outcome isn't that important to you.

Combining talking style and strategy leads to excellence in almost any situation. To develop sound communication tactics, keep five points in mind.

1. **STAY GROUNDED.** Being a positive force requires getting yourself together. Know what you stand for in life.
2. **COOPERATE.** People get power through cooperation and service. Working together creates synergy, influence, and capacity.
3. **SIMPLIFY.** Live simply. Don't look for the benefits of more. Realize that by having enough you are truly rich.
4. **SHAPE IT.** Master things by letting them go their own way.

Don't interfere; rather, shape things as they come to fit a grounded way of life.

5. **LET IT GO.** Do your best then let go of results. Harboring anger, animosity, or grief over what transpires in a conversation anchors you at that spot. No growth takes place till you move on.

Remember to seek excellence not success. Strategies built on "winning at all cost" may prove successful today but plant the seeds for ultimate failure.

Working on style and strategies that develop and highlight personal excellence makes the best possible you. That improvement will stay with you whether the conversation is successful or not.

PERSONAL GROWTH

IMPROVING YOUR SPEAKING ABILITY

Preparing to improve

THIS CHAPTER FOCUSES ON IMPROVING YOU. Not changing you but taking your talents and skills and shaping them so they help you build speaking excellence.

How can we get there?

Let's return to the idea of approaching English-speaking improvement as a world-class athlete. An athlete in a specific sport such as basketball studies how they can succeed with their specific talents.

A tall person sees an advantage in refining skills such as rebounding and short shots to make them a more effective player. A shorter, quicker player works on dribbling, passing, and long-range shooting to maximize potential.

The keys involve being honest with who you are, what your skills are, and working to take advantage of them. Great athletes realize that if they focus on excellence then winning will take care of itself.

Start with you

Life pops when a person maximizes potential. This requires not only identifying and incorporating talents and skills but working to improve problem areas that hinder maximum growth.

Let's start working on reaching your full potential.

A basketball player who wants to improve may say:

- "I want to shoot better so I'm going to take 500 practice shots a day."
- "My rebounding needs improvement so I'm going to practice against the tallest players I can find."
- "Dribbling is causing me problems so I'm going to take a basketball and bounce it everywhere I go."

The athlete sees an issue and attacks the problem with specific drills to improve the skillset. Speaking English is no different.

TOP TIP
REALIZE WHO YOU ARE, IDENTIFY STRENGTHS AND WEAKNESSES, AND WORK ON IMPROVING THEM.

This chapter provides two tools to identify and improve your English-speaking strengths and weaknesses, the *Talking Improvement Plan* (TIP) and the *Personal Talking Brand* (PTB).

These two easy-to-use programs work by maximizing your potential as an English speaker much like the training regimen of the world-class athlete.

Change review

Before introducing the TIP and the PTB let's review the key points to improve your English-speaking ability.

Positive change takes place when you:

1. **BELIEVE.** Believe in your dream. Visualize the change, see a new you. Avoid comments such as "I'd like to…" that sound as if you've already quit.
2. **START BEING.** Real change takes place when you start being instead of doing. "I am an English speaker" not "I want to be a good English speaker."
3. **PAY ATTENTION.** Be mindful of your words and actions as an "English speaker." Pay attention to the things that come out of your mouth.

4. **SEEK BALANCE.** Seek speaking balance, accepting the positive and negative emotions within you. Don't hide.
5. **GIVE IN.** When facing a difficulty, give in to it. Denying speaking problems prevents growth. Don't expect them to magically disappear. Work to improve.
6. **LISTEN TO TEACHERS.** People who point out faults are your most benevolent teachers. Don't take criticism as an insult but learn from it. People may be clumsy or rude when criticizing, but listen and learn.
7. **CORRECT PROBLEMS.** Correct your problems. Own your challenges. Don't blame others.
8. **STEP BACK.** Do the work then step back. The road to serenity lies in effort and acceptance. Don't brag or boast but just do the work and let it go when done. People notice improvement.
9. **DWELL IN REALITY.** Dwell in reality. Let illusions go. Understand and accept today, not yesterday or tomorrow.

How to use this chapter's tools

This chapter introduces the Talking Improvement Plan (TIP) and the Personal Talking Brand (PTB). Read through the ideas and goals of the plans in the following pages.

Once finished, refer to the Appendix where a blank copy of each plan allows you to create your own improvement plan.

Talking Improvement Plan (TIP)

1. Assess the way you speak
2. Identify strengths and weaknesses
3. Consider potential strategies
4. Make a plan
5. Track your progress

Improvement requires assessing skills and developing a strategy to work on strengths and weaknesses. The Talking Improvement Plan (TIP) focuses on you and your talking style. The objective is gradual improvement so that skills and confidence build at a sustainable pace.

The five-step TIP devises a personalized ongoing strategy to fine-tune English-speaking abilities.

The system provides specific individualized focal points for day-to-day speaking activities. These strategies become part of daily speech within a short period of time as you start to be instead of do.

So let's go through each of the five TIP steps.

Step 1: Assess your speech

The first step requires an assessment of the way you speak. This provides a baseline to know where to focus efforts. This step involves answering fifteen questions regarding your personal talking style.

The key to these questions is to be as honest as possible. Think about speaking situations that cause you problems. Where did you struggle? What speaking areas make you feel unconfident?

Look in the book's Appendix for the questions.

Step 2: Identify strengths and weaknesses

Go over your answers from Step One then move onto the questions in Step Two. These will help identify areas of strength and weakness when talking to others.

As the athlete, it's essential to be aware of things you do well AND not so well.

Humans tend to focus on only their best or worst traits. A person who only focuses on poor skills or habits leads to a poor self-image while one who only focuses on good traits erroneously inflates their ego by ignoring problems.

Yinyang teaches to accept all emotions or traits as one. Don't view yourself like a buffet dinner where you pick only certain items and not others.

Again, look in the Appendix for the tools.

Step 3: Consider potential strategies

This step examines potential strategies for areas of English-speaking strength and weakness.

The blank TIP in the Appendix has a quick reference guide to rank problem areas and provide potential suggestions.

Here we'll go into greater detail on how to improve in specific speaking areas.

Mindful tips

This section contains potential strategies on improving individual aspects of talking by using mindfulness. Be mindful of both strengths and weaknesses. Both elements are essential when developing an improvement plan.

Top-notch speakers maintain an awareness of what they're saying, why they're saying it, and how they're saying it. They master all physical and mental aspects. This requires the ability to simultaneously operate your brain, face, sound, movement, and listening skills.

"If you hear a voice within that says 'you cannot paint' then by all means paint and that voice will be silenced."

Vincent Van Gogh

Gradual focus, gradual improvement

World-class athletes use two types of tips on improving a technique.

1. **PRACTICE IN PRIVATE**: Athletes build muscle memory by privately practicing certain motions in slow motion. Do the same by practicing facial expressions, gestures, and other speaking techniques when alone.
2. **PRACTICE IN PUBLIC**: An athlete will incorporate one or two tips into a performance. Using more than one or two tips causes confusion. Once they are ingrained then add more.

For example, a private-speaking tip for eye contact involves using a mirror to practice. A public-speaking tip would be to concentrate on using eye contact every thirty seconds during a conversation.

Don't worry if incorporating changes into your talking style cause slight disruptions or awkwardness in the smooth flow of conversation. Conversation partners won't notice slight pauses but increased eye contact or a more animated you will impress them!

Suggestion guide

Suggestions are categorized as either:

1. Suggestions practiced in private or

2. Suggestions used in conversation

TIP suggestions on improving English speaking

1. SPEED: TIPS FOR TALKING TOO FAST OR TOO SLOW

a. (2) Too fast. Practice starting slower. Focus on slowing down the first three words of each new burst of conversation. Practice by carefully pronouncing each word instead of rushing to make a point.

b. (2) Too fast. Stop to breathe between paragraphs, ideas, and natural breaks. Use pauses to build drama and gather thoughts.

c. (2) Too fast. Don't ramble. Focus conversation on one to three points and then let the other person speak.

d. (1) Too fast/too slow. Record yourself on a mobile device. Pick a topic such as family, school, or work and freely speak for one minute. Convert it to a written word format to check the speed. A range of 170 to 190 words per minute should be the goal.

e. General tips:
    - Be mindful of the power of slowly building up to a key point
    - Be mindful of the conversation path and avoid unnecessary detours. Stay on point.
    - Be mindful of clearly pronouncing each word.
    - Notice impatience or frustration in listeners.

2. VOLUME: TIPS FOR SPEAKING TOO LOUD OR TOO SOFT

a. (1) Too loud/too soft. Take a mobile device and set it on record.

Place the device on a table and walk five steps away. Give a 30-second impromptu talk about family, school, or work in a normal conversational tone. Listen to the recording. What do you hear? Screaming or mumbling? Practice changing the distance and volume to fit varying situations such as individual, group, and public presentations. Try it with music playing to mimic party or group settings. Can you be heard? Do you jump out of the recording like a bang?

b. (1) Too soft. Go outside and scream as loud as possible. Listen to the scream. Realize that you do have a loud voice.

c. (2) Too soft. Stand tall with shoulders back and head and chin held slightly up. Bring the words up from the stomach not just the throat.

d. (2) Too loud. Notice how people respond to you. If they back up or cut conversations short, then you need to tone it down.

e. General tips:

- Be mindful of posture. Standing tall with shoulders back improves volume.
- Be mindful of others' reactions. If they step back, lower your voice. If they continually ask "What?" or move closer, speak up.
- Be mindful of where the words are coming from, the stomach or the throat.

3. HAND GESTURES: TIPS FOR TOO MANY OR TOO FEW

a. (1) Too many or too few. Be mindful of hands during conversation. Concentrate on using only one hand gesture or body movement at a time. Use the gesture to punctuate the most important point. Don't overdo them.

b. (1) Too many/too few. Give a one-minute impromptu talk in front of a mirror. Think about using two separate gestures while making key points. The gestures can be a shrug of the shoulders, a wave of the hand, a fist pounding the open palm of the other hand, hands above the head in celebration, or two hands with palms out signifying someone should stop.

c.   (2) Too many. Be mindful of tendencies to wildly flail arms in conversation. Excited speakers use their arms too much, causing spilled drinks, inadvertent punches of others standing near, and nervous listeners. Don't extend the arms outside of the shoulders for the majority of gestures unless making a public presentation. Slowly make grand gestures.

4. FACIAL EXPRESSIONS: TIPS FOR TOO MANY OR TOO FEW

a.   (1) Too many/too few. Again, give a one-minute impromptu speech in front of a mirror giving a self-introduction to a new acquaintance. Tell the imaginary person who you are and include information about your hometown, education, and family. Give the talk as normally as possible. Then give it a second time and concentrate on improving facial expressions. Start the talk with a smile and then use whatever expressions necessary to complement the content.

b.   (2) Too many. Many people wear uneasy emotions on their faces. This impedes communication by sending bad signals to the other person. Start conversations with a slight smile or neutral facial expression. Avoid excessive expressions such as anger, sadness, wincing, sneering, and pouting. When emotions take over try to return to a neutral face.

c.   (2) Too few. Speakers who never show any facial emotion send a message of indifference to the listener. If facial expressions prove challenging, then practice incorporating a slight smile into greetings and when listening.

d. (2) Expression. Notice the expression on your face when you pass a mirror. What does it say? Does it encourage or repel?

e. Practice starting every conversation with a neutral or slight smile. Obviously a big smile in most conversations is even better.

5. EYE CONTACT: TIPS FOR TOO MUCH OR TOO LITTLE

a. (2) Too much/too little. Eye contact is tricky. A fine line exists between too much and too little. Greetings and goodbyes involve looking the other person in the eyes. Be mindful of this act.

b. (2) Too much/too little with two people. The positions of two or more bodies play a role in eye contact. Two people driving in a car or walking cannot have much eye contact. Consider the physical situation.

c. (2) Too much/too little in a presentation. Public presentations provide an opportunity to effectively use eye contact. Look individual audience members in the eyes when speaking. This engages listeners and calms you when nervous by focusing on one person instead of the whole audience. Speakers who avoid eye contact appear aloof or nervous.

d. (2) Too much. Staring deeply into another's eyes can cause discomfort or embarrassment because it can be considered an invasion of privacy. Be mindful if a long gaze into another's eyes causes uneasiness. If it does, then avoid doing it.

e. (2) Too little. Totally avoiding eye contact sends a message of shyness, guilt, or disdain. Good communicators realize the importance of creating a connection with the listener through eye contact. In a regular conversation, try to create eye contact a minimum of 3 to 5 times per minute.

f. General tips:

- Be mindful of eye contact and its impact. Use it to punctuate an important point in conjunction with appropriate hand gestures.

- Use eye contact saying hello and good bye.
- Be mindful of the careful balance between too much and too little eye contact.
- Try to make eye contact with each person when talking to a small group of people.

6. TOUCH: TIPS FOR TOO MUCH OR TOO LITTLE

a. (1) Too much/too little. Deal carefully when touching another person while talking. Some cultures find it offensive and others find it necessary. In dealing with other cultures, know the customs and practice appropriate measures.

b. (2) Too much/too little. Inappropriate touching is never acceptable. The best advice for meeting an attractive person is HANDS OFF.

c. (2) Too much/too little. Situations dictate when touching may be appropriate. Acceptable ways include offering a hand to someone getting out of a car, opening a door, or greeting someone. Touching someone lightly on their elbow to get their attention can be used. Avoid aggressive hands-on approaches like back slapping, hugging, kissing, and pats on the arm with anyone other than relatives or friends unless it is culturally expected.

d. Shaking hands. Shaking hands is all over the board. Some cultures shake hands while others don't. Some cultures only men shake hands while women don't. Be aware of local customs if possible.

e. General tips:

- Be mindful of who you are talking with and of cultural preferences when it comes to touching.
- Be mindful that touching someone repeatedly or suggestively is wrong and may cause serious problems.

- Be mindful of kind acts that involve touching, such as helping someone out of a chair. Keep the touch light.
- Be mindful of relatives and close friends who may expect a physical act such as a hug or a kiss on the cheek. Try to be smooth and not make the act awkward or inappropriate.

7. DISTANCE: TIPS ON BEING TOO CLOSE OR TOO FAR AWAY

a. (1) Too close/too far. Again, culture plays an important role in determining distance. Try to be aware of the customs and practice appropriate measures.

b. (2) Too close. Standing too close intrudes on personal space. You may think it sends a positive sign of fraternity, but others may find it offensive. Be mindful of body language and act appropriately by creating a comfortable space, approximately an arm's length away.

c. (2) Too far. Standing more than two feet away sends a signal of distrust or fear. Again, create a comfortable space approximately an arm's length away.

8. INTERRUPTIONS: TIPS FOR TOO MANY

Too few interruptions do not create a problem.

a. (2) Too many. Interruptions rudely disturb a person's attempt to talk. However, we all do it. Some speakers go on and on and won't stop talking until we stop them. Other speakers have facts wrong, requiring a correction. Be mindful when interrupting another speaker. Ask "Is this necessary, or do I just want to be the center of attention?"

b. (2) Too many. When interrupting another speaker, apologize and explain the reason for the interruption. Apologizing brings attention to a bad habit and may slowly stop it.

c. General tips:

- Be mindful of how many interruptions you make during a conversation.
- Be mindful of the reasons for interrupting another speaker.
- Always apologize when interrupting another speaker.

9. LISTENING: TIPS FOR TOO MUCH OR TOO LITTLE

a. (1) Active listening. Practice mindful listening to the television, radio, or Internet. Listen carefully and think up questions for the announcer.

b. (2) Too little listening. Focus on the speaker and practice asking at least one question.

c. (2) Too little listening. How often do you respond to another person by talking about yourself? Realize that thinking about you instead of paying attention to the other person shows a lack of character and imagination.

d. (2) Too much listening. Too much listening says you're not talking at all. Show life by incorporating what you've heard into a question on a regular basis.

e. General tips:

- Be mindful by focusing on the speaker.
- Avoid making your inner and outer dialogue all about you. Listening requires thinking about others.
- Use active listening.

10. PRONUNCIATION: TIPS

a. (1) Practice saying mispronounced words. Many websites provide audio pronunciation of words. Listen to and practice troublesome words.

b. (2) Avoid saying mispronounced words in public until your skills improve.

c.   (2) People's names cause pronunciation problems. Do not be shy in asking a person to repeat the pronunciation of their name. Say it to them to judge correctness.

d.   (1) Dealing with other cultures and unfamiliar words causes problems. Again, practice often-used words or ask for help. People from other cultures appreciate the effort to communicate in their language or to at least say their name correctly so try. Effort shows respect.

11. TRANSITIONS: HOW TO CHANGE A CONVERSATION

a.   (2) Changing a conversation topic takes mindfulness and, possibly, courage. Prepare an interesting point or ask a relevant question when changing topics.

b.   (2) Use a standard phrase to shift a conversation topic such as "that reminds of something," "while I am talking to you I have something I want to discuss," "Something's been bothering me that I want to talk about," and "Hey, did you hear about...?"

c.   General tips:

- Be mindful of natural breaks in a conversation that allow a topic shift. Don't change topics in midstream unless necessary due to time or emergency. Be patient.

- Don't start a conversation in an accusatory tone. Putting someone on the defensive immediately creates a hostile atmosphere. Use a transition to ease into challenging conversations such as "There is something we need to discuss."

12. CROWDS: TIPS FOR TALKING WITH LARGE NUMBERS OF PEOPLE

a.   (2) The only way to get comfortable talking to a large audience is by doing it. The more you practice, the easier it gets. If talking in front of people makes you nervous, then start with a few people, maybe four or five at lunch. Practicing with smaller groups increases confidence. When nervous about an upcoming presentation get a few friends together and practice beforehand.

b. (2) Personalize topics so that you're speaking to each individual in an audience. Focus attention on individuals in the audience (especially friends or encouraging faces) and not the entire audience.

c. (1) Don't memorize speeches. Have an outline and any specific points ready. Refer to these as necessary. Remember the audience doesn't know the speech.

d. (2) Remember physical actions. Stand tall, breathe deeply, pause when necessary, script a few hand gestures into the speech, and smile.

e. General tips:
- Be mindful of the individual when speaking to an audience.
- Be mindful of friends and encouraging people who are present.
- Refer to notes when necessary. Keep the notes and speech at the same place in case you need to refer to the notes. Flipping through notes reveals an unprepared speaker.
- Be mindful of breathing.
- Tell a story don't give a speech.

13. TELLING STORIES: TIPS ON ENTERTAINING AN AUDIENCE

a. (1) Practice telling a story or a joke in front of a mirror then to one or two people. Ask them if they enjoyed it and where you might improve. Practice till you perfect it.

b. (2) Wait for the right time. Don't force a joke or story before the audience is ready. Every good storyteller knows the importance of timing.

c. (2) Have the audience's attention. Make sure the audience is ready to listen. Use a strong voice, vary pitch and volume, have an animated face, and use hand gestures to grab attention.

d. (2) Go all out. Don't tell a story without enthusiasm or style.

e. (1) Watch good storytellers on the internet. The internet's TED Talks series has numerous speakers who do excellent work at entertaining audiences. Watch a few and take cues from the speakers.

f. General tips:

-   Be mindful of the timing of when to tell a story.
-   Be mindful of the physical nature of a presentation.
-   Control and use your energy. An energetic storyteller lights up an audience.
-   Slowly build a story. Don't rush to the end, especially a punch line in a joke.

14. GOOD CHARACTER: TIPS ON SPEAKING WITH STRENGTH AND CONFIDENCE

a. (1) Study what excellent character means and then focus on having it in conversations.

b. (2) Always strive for authentic, open, supportive, and honest conversation. If you cannot be honest and supportive (even in disagreement), then say nothing at all.

15. CONFRONTATIONS: TIPS FOR DEALING WITH EMOTIONAL CONVERSATIONS

a. (2) Maintain composure by breathing deeply. Stop to think before flying off the handle. Remember people mimic who they're talking to so if you get mad then they will too.

b. (1) Visualize the conversation before it comes. Know key points and stick to them.

    c.   (2) Relax when you don't understand something. Be calm, quiet, and aware. Don't try too hard.

    d.   Your best weapon is intelligence not emotion.

16. VOCABULARY: TIPS FOR IMPROVING THE WORDS YOU USE

    a.   (1) Focus on your area of work or interest by researching and practicing popular or often-used vocabulary words.

    b.   (2) Don't force newly-learned words into conversations. Try to incorporate them naturally. Keep them to a minimum, using only one or two new words per conversation.

Step 4: Make a plan

Write a short plan for improving speaking skills by focusing on two areas of speech, a weakness and strength.

> **"You learn from things that don't go well, and try to capitalize when they do. You build on those strengths and try to make your weaknesses stronger."**
>
> **Gary Sinese**

Setting too many improvement goals at one time can be just as counterproductive as not setting any goals. TIP's goal-setting strategy focuses on one weak point and one strong point at a time.

Write down one skill you do well and one that needs work. Then look at the suggestions in Step Three. Which suggestions do you think might help improve your strength and weakness? Write the suggestion down and begin practicing.

Great athletes, actors, and businesspeople realize which strengths make them successful. They also understand the importance of working on areas of weakness.

TIP capitalizes on both strengths and weaknesses. Strive for excellence. Let's look at an example.

1. **STRENGTH**: I am good at telling stories. Plan: Work on developing one really good story that can be told at dinner or a party. Practice enhancing with hand gestures, facial expressions, and sounds. Work on not just entertaining but wowing an audience.
2. **WEAKNESS**: I talk too fast. Plan: Be mindful of taking a deep breath before every conversation and think "take it slow."

Another example:

1. **STRENGTH**: I am a good listener. Plan: Concentrate on using active listening in all business settings.
2. **WEAKNESS**: I can't make eye contact. Plan: Practice looking at yourself when passing a mirror. Say hello quietly to yourself. Do it until you feel comfortable; then try it on friends or family.

Make your plans easy to remember and fun to do.

After two weeks of concentrating on a strength and weakness, track your progress and determine if it's time to focus on two new areas. Continue on this plan of attack until you are satisfied with your improvement.

Step 5: Track your progress

After working on one strong point and one weak point for two weeks determine if sufficient progress has been made to move onto other areas.

To determine progress answer the questions in Step Five. Again, be honest in assessing your progress.

If you believe sufficient progress has been achieved, then start working on another topic area. If not then further work is required. As with any effort to change, your honest appraisal is necessary.

TIP conclusion

The Talking Improvement Plan (TIP) is an opportunity to improve specific strong and weak English-speaking areas. As with any change, the amount of time devoted determines the amount of improvement.

We have provided a blank TIP in the Appendix of this book. Go through the process, target the areas that will advance your English, and work on improving with our easy-to-do suggestions.

If you are ready then go to the Appendix and complete the TIP.

Refer back to this chapter for more detail if necessary when using the TIP. Best of luck!

Personal Talking Brand (PTB)

Successful people understand the importance of projecting the right image at the right time. This requires "putting it all together" including speaking skill, appropriate content, dress, and manners.

Keep in mind that "putting it all together" differs greatly for a Wall

Street attorney, a jazz musician, and first grade teacher. Each has an individual image that they seek to project to clients, audiences, or students. The individual determines their image.

Successful people get an edge on competitors by consciously considering their public image. They work to project the right image through words and actions.

Today image consultants call this effort personal branding. Whether you realize it or not, you have a personal brand and customers.

Personal branding: The practice of people marketing themselves and their careers as brands to distinguish themselves from rivals in the eyes of the customer.

Yes, you have customers. Each day people decide whether to "buy" the product of you! People determine if they want to "buy" you whether it's applying for a job, talking at a party, or making a presentation. How do you convince others the investment in you is worth it?

How do you come off when interacting with others? Like a television commercial for a new automobile, a tragic news story, a blank wall, or a cartoon character?

TOP TIP
STRIVE FOR EXCELLENCE IN PROJECTING SKILL, COMPETENCE AND PROPER IMAGE TO CUSTOMERS.

What's your brand?

Talking comes in all styles. Fast, slow, excited, determined, and sexy to name just a few. What's your brand of talking?

Focusing on your personal style or brand of speaking creates an opportunity for improvement. Our emotions ebb and flow, but each of us relies on a basic pattern of talking that reflects our personality.

Determining your style and improving it increases chances for excellence.

Authentic consistency

Nobody likes a phony. People who try to be someone they're not are easy to spot and even easier to dislike. This book's goal is to make better speakers, not frauds.

Creating and maintaining a personal talking brand is a never-ending circular process. People change throughout life and must continually reexamine and modify their speaking style and strategies. Do you still talk like a 14-year-old valley girl as a 40-year-old executive? Have you received a promotion and now have more responsibility? Maybe it's time to change!

The four keys to developing a personal talking brand are:

Self-definition	**Authenticity**
Transparency	**Accountability**

These four elements make up the continuing process of developing and updating a personal brand. Here is the process.

Personal Talking Brand circular process

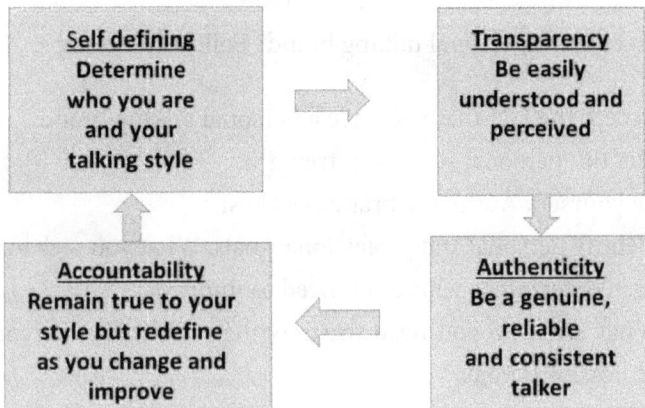

Self defining Determine who you are and your talking style	→	Transparency Be easily understood and perceived
Accountability Remain true to your style but redefine as you change and improve	←	Authenticity Be a genuine, reliable and consistent talker

The process is like the cyclical nature of the four seasons. The spring sees the seedlings of growth sprout into who you are and what you stand for. The summer season brings transparency as all now see a strong, growing, talking brand. The autumn brings harvest and an excellent crop from your genuine, reliable, and consistent work. The winter brings solitude and the beginning of the regeneration of an improved you who will come forward in the spring.

Everyone is unique. The first steep step in branding involves a self-defining examination. Who are you? What do you stand for? How do people perceive you? How do your words reflect the true you?

The self-definition step forward encourages transparency, which leads to a more authentic you.

"Authenticity is the alignment of head, mouth, heart and feet—feeling, saying, thinking and doing the same thing—consistently. This builds trust, and followers love leaders they can trust."

Lance Secretan

Creating a personal talking brand

How do you create a personal talking brand? Follow these steps:

1. Accept the fact that you have a personal talking brand.
2. Identify personal speaking strengths.
3. Be yourself. Authentic brands sell best.
4. Identify personal and professional goals. What you seek to accomplish determines where you need to improve.
5. What areas do you need to strengthen to achieve personal and professional goals?
6. Identify your emotional appeal. What stands out about the way you talk? Sense of humor, intensity, or kindness? You name it.
7. Describe why people enjoy talking with you. What is your specialty? What do you do best when talking to others?

Consider these two questions:

•   Do your personal and professional goals match up with your skills?
•   How can you improve to achieve sustained excellence?

Each professional and personal goal requires unique skills. If you want to be an attorney but have trouble speaking in public then you have work to do much like a tall basketball player who can't rebound.

A personal talking brand requires honesty. You may want to be an extrovert but friends consider you shy. Personal branding identifies strengths and weaknesses to build on so you can achieve personal and professional goals.

The concept of a talking brand strikes some as crass but I believe everyone from a reclusive artist to a shy 16-year-old burnishes a personal talking brand. Taking control of your brand allows for conscious decisions on how to improve.

Personal talking styles

"To thine own self be true, and it must follow, as the night the day, Thou canst not then be false to any man."

William Shakespeare

To promote the best in you requires knowledge of how to talk. What personal talking habits drive your brand? What do others see as your strengths? Or as the quote below states, what do you stand for?

"When we're talking about brand, we're talking about what does the brand stand for?"

John Quelch

When you talk, what do you stand for?

Review the standard list of talking types. Which ones are you? Keep in mind many people are a blend of several types.

Standard talking styles

1. **PLANNER**. Meticulously plans what to say
2. **MANIPULATOR**. Uses words to get ahead of others
3. **LEADER**. Person born to lead others
4. **DEBATER**. Wants to discuss merits of all issues
5. **CHANGE AGENT.** Wants to change status quo
6. **PROBLEM SOLVER**. Can fix problems involving people/things
7. **FIGHTER**. Always ready to defend a cause at all costs
8. **FREE SPIRIT**. Fun, energetic, and happy

9. **LOGICAL**. Practical, quiet, and reliable

10. **PROTECTOR**. Warm defender of home and family

11. **BOSS**. Administrative type who's always managing

12. **HELPER**. Popular and kind; always busy helping

13. **RECLUSE**. Shies away from conversation and people

14. **EXCITEMENT SEEKER**. Fast-paced and looking for new challenges

15. **ENTREPRENEUR**. Lives on the edge; full of business ideas

16. **ENTERTAINER**. The life of the party

17. **TEACHER**. Always giving lessons to others

18. **RAMBLER**. Goes in all directions with no warning of change

Who are you? Are you one style or a blend of several?

- **Action activity:** Watch famous people speak on the news or Internet. Notice how their personality, whether exciting, boring, or logical, fits their speaking style. Successful individuals understand how to deliver a complete well-wrapped package to their consumers.

- **Shared activity:** Work with a friend on developing a personal brand for each other. Focus on what speaking traits best serve to highlight each other's personality strengths.

Question of the day

Talk about the following question with a friend or form your own opinion. Read the conversation between Emmett, Iris and Edie then consider how you would respond. Remember to say why you feel or think as you do.

Question: What if my personal talking brand doesn't fit my career goal?

- **Emmett:** People need to be realistic about the future. Just because you want to become an actress or lawyer doesn't mean you have the appropriate speaking skills. Developing a personal brand makes you accept who you are and gives you a more realistic shot at success.
- **Iris:** People change. I was a shy kid but now I talk all the time. A personal talking brand is a valuable tool, but it changes as I do. As I improve my skills, my chances for success increase and my personal brand becomes more powerful, telling a new story about me. I'm playing the lead character in my own life's story.
- **Edie:** I'm driven to succeed and will do whatever it takes to win. I'll use any talking style necessary to achieve a goal. I may not be great at it but that won't stop me from trying. People don't always know what to expect from me but I don't care. Winning is all that matters.

What do you think? Should you focus on a realistic picture, dream big, or try to win at all cost?

Developing a personal talking brand

A blank Personal Talking Brand (PTB) is located in the Appendix. Answer the questions to develop your own personal talking brand. Remember to dwell in reality, while pushing for personal excellence.

Using your PTB

Keep your PTB in mind when involved in conversations. Focus on your strengths when talking to others while continuing to work on the areas needing improvement to achieve personal and professional goals.

Conclusion

Personal and professional growth requires work. This section provides the tools to change how you communicate which lays the groundwork for excellence.

Realize only you decide whether to strive for excellence or muddle along hoping things will magically fall into place for you.

If you are ready then go to the Appendix and fill out your Personal Talking Brand.

Nothing works till you do.

SPEAKING TIPS

366 SPEAKING SUGGESTIONS

THIS CHAPTER CONTAINS ENOUGH SPEAKING and life tips to last a year or more! Use the 366 tips to improve speaking balance, strength, and character.

366 speaking tips

1. Always think before speaking.
2. Practice active listening.
3. Work for excellence not success.
4. Do what's right rather than say what's right.
5. Be open and attentive rather than a slave to an agenda.
6. Let go of the fantasy of what might have been.
7. If you try too hard, then you often achieve the opposite.
8. Breathe when speaking.
9. Stand tall or sit upright when speaking in public.
10. Ask for what you want in a polite but firm tone.
11. Turn others' comments into questions.
12. Silence is a great source of strength.
13. Character requires the ability to say "yes" and "no."
14. Impact an outcome by using a talking strategy.
15. Use hand gestures when making a point.
16. Don't flail arms and hands like a stranded motorist.
17. Be authentic.
18. Well versed, not overly opinionated.
19. Speaking practice improves strength and confidence.
20. Focus on timing when telling a joke or story.
21. Choose talking over social media posts.
22. Listen to what you say.
23. Acknowledge and accept who you are.

24. Protect and defend all humans' right to speak.

25. Encourage others to improve their speaking skills.

26. Time and money spent improving speaking skills pays off.

27. Focus on good character when speaking.

28. Relax if you cannot understand someone. Be calm, quiet, aware.

29. Change what you can, accept the rest.

30. Muscle memory overcomes fear and builds strength. Practice.

31. Action leads to more action, both positive and negative.

32. Everybody's opinion matters to them. Respect others' words.

33. Visualize successful conversations.

34. Leaders work for both self-interest and relationship-building.

35. To influence others, get yourself together.

36. Relaxed, not rigid.

37. A leader's clarity sets the tone. Be clear, not muddled.

38. A great ego doesn't make a great person. Stay humble.

39. Character builds one sentence at a time.

40. Don't cling to good points made in conversation.

41. Conversation, not control. Talk, don't tell.

42. How matters as much as what when talking. Think physical as well as mental.

43. Seek balance in conversations.

44. Patient storytellers build drama.

45. Champions practice until they get it right.

46. Nothing works until you do. Get to work on a goal.

47. Choose advancing the cause of all over winning alone.

48. Regret frightens more than failure. Try.

49. Observant, not obnoxious.

50. Talking takes two people.

51. Grab an audience's attention with silence.

52. Dig the well before you're thirsty. Plan today.

53. Silence reveals the mind of a group. Learn to read the emptiness.

54. A leader allows things to happen and then shapes them as they come.

55. Stick to the point when disagreeing.

56. Don't fear growing slowly; fear not growing at all.

57. Speak with the same grace and ease as the talented dancer. Hear the music, get the beat.

58. Raise a sail one foot to get 10 feet of wind.

59. Listeners hear and feel comments. Work on creating good feelings.

60. Instead of pointing at someone, point straight up.

61. Use "I feel…" instead of "You always…"

62. A true leader is both fighter and healer.

63. Keep hands and paper away from the mouth when talking.

64. Demonstrate, don't explain.

65. Use facial expressions like an actor.

66. Make eye contact at least 3-5 times per minute.

67. Use individual eye contact when speaking to an audience.

68. Vary tone and volume for effect.

69. Today, not yesterday or tomorrow.

70. Forcing people gets results, but they may be upset and plot revenge.

71. The universe is inclusive. Don't accept one person and not another.

72. Your face tells a story. Don't let it be an ugly one.

73. He who asks is a fool for a moment, but he who doesn't remains a fool.

74. Clever not crude.

75. Avoid consistent inner and outer dialogues about you.

76. Not considering others hurts future opportunities.

77. Emphasize similarities when making acquaintances.

78. Don't cling to comfort. Growth requires change.

79. You can't make an angry group happy. Let them fight it out.

80. Is your conversation interruption necessary? Really?

81. Speaking excellence requires consistent effort.

82. Don't let others' words or tears dissuade a conviction. Be fair but firm.

83. Talk about what other people enjoy.

84. Nod for positive reaction but avoid negative gestures.

85. Ask a question to keep the conversation going.

86. Avoid yawning when talking to others.

87. Emphasize the most important word in a sentence for maximum impact.

88. Self-centered comments are dull as dishwater.

89. Thoughtful not thoughtless.

90. Keep calm when verbally threatened.

91. Stretch vowels to emphasize words.

92. Water is soft but overcomes the hard.

93. Count your interruptions during conversations, the fewer the better.

94. Use eye contact saying hello or good bye.

95. Build speaking strengths and improve weaknesses.

96. Whenever possible, smile when starting a conversation.

97. Polite, not pompous.

98. Write a plan today to improve speaking skills.

99. Go all out. You can't tell a great story half-way.

100. Monotone sound went out in the 1960s…vary tones.

101. Learn to see backwards, inside-out, and upside-down.

102. Pause for emphasis.

103. When you're not practicing, someone else is getting better.

104. Live communication beats social media words.

105. Strong conversation doesn't require muscles or a big mouth.

106. Consistent, confident character is the goal in speaking.

107. People love thoughtful conversation.

108. Be firm when telling someone bad news.

109. Stunning, not stupid.

110. Don't seek others' approval. Just be grounded.

111. English's most important sentence: "Hello. How are you?"

112. Tender not tense.

113. You never get a second chance to make a first impression.

114. Practice difficult or foreign food words.

115. Conversation mirrors thoughts.

116. Hostile atmospheres create defensive people.

117. Respond, don't reject.

118. "Off-the-wall" questions grab attention.

119. Dignity, not revenge, when hearing bad news.

120. Start with small groups if audiences make you nervous.

121. Plan key points in important conversations.

122. Sports and politics don't build character, they reveal it.

123. Prepare topics for the next party conversation.

124. Small details reveal an individual. Examine yours.

125. Tell a story don't give a speech.

126. If you blame, then there is no end to the blaming.

127. Be patient for the right moment to speak.

128. Arms folded across the chest send a "closed" signal.

129. Avoiding eye contact says "I don't want to be here."

130. Ask for the right to apologize.

131. Anger feeds on fear. Be strong in its face.

132. Tasteful not tawdry.

133. Practice speaking clearly.

134. Realize how much little will do.

135. People appreciate grateful conversations.

136. Fortune favors the prepared mind.

137. Authentic not obnoxious.

138. Practice slowing down your conversation.

139. Liars eventually pay a price.
140. Don't be a grump.
141. Let others know about hurtful comments.
142. Don't monopolize conversations no matter how much you love to talk.
143. Don't slur words; carefully pronounce.
144. Greet people by name; ask if necessary.
145. Use positive body language all day.
146. Nothing is permanent. Friends come and go.
147. Encourage friends to seek excellence.
148. True simplicity is not easy.
149. Keep a sense of humor when receiving backhanded compliments.
150. Weakness of attitude becomes weakness of character.
151. Don't overwhelm new friends with excessive conversation.
152. Everybody loves a compliment. Give a few today.
153. Don't ramble on…focus.
154. Don't give phony-sounding compliments.
155. No backhanded compliments like "that was smart for a change."
156. Base compliments in fact, not on glossed-over deficiencies.
157. Smile when giving compliments but don't laugh.
158. Get to the point; no long-drawn-out requests.
159. Open not judgmental.
160. Knowledge gives power; character gives respect.
161. Compliment action, not looks.
162. If receiving praise drives you, then you'll never be happy.
163. Set the right tone in conversations.
164. Think being, not doing.
165. A stiff apology is a second insult.
166. Don't expect praise for giving a compliment.

167. Record yourself talking and critique.

168. Invitation details include who, what, when, where, and what to bring.

169. Apologize when interrupting a speaker.

170. Accept "no" like an adult.

171. Invite in private, not in front of others who are not invited.

172. Breathe to regain balance.

173. Respond to positive comments; ignore negative portions.

174. Respond enthusiastically when accepting an invitation.

175. Don't be wishy-washy when declining an invitation.

176. Positive words ripple through family, community, nation, world, and universe.

177. Kind not curt.

178. Move on when someone repeatedly declines invitations.

179. Encourage people when declining an invitation.

180. Keep your word when accepting an invitation.

181. Avoid name-dropping.

182. Apologize when late no matter who you are or what happened.

183. A leader's touch is light.

184. Arrogance creates enemies. Be respectful.

185. Don't force or dominate; lead.

186. Don't be a "know-it-all."

187. Have at least one good clean story or joke to tell.

188. In conflict, be fair and generous.

189. Make only one point at a time in back-and-forth conversations.

190. People may need time to think about what you said or asked.

191. Don't be afraid to ask again if someone said no once before.

192. Public speaking is human's number one fear, so you're not alone.

193. Don't expect to be perfect when talking. Take risks, make mistakes.

194. Ask if you can give advice before doing so.

195. Arrogant people avoid eye contact.

196. Being nervous means you want to do well. It's OK.

197. Inspired, not irksome.

198. Practice important talks by recording and analyzing.

199. Audiences can rarely spot a nervous speaker.

200. Having power tests character. Don't fail the test.

201. Gossiping is mean.

202. Just say "thank you" to ignorant advice.

203. Don't read a speech; prepare an outline.

204. A good speaking goal is 150 to 200 spoken words per minute.

205. PowerPoint presentations can be really boring.

206. Shaking a reputation as a gossip is tough.

207. Know your audience.

208. Natural breaks in conversation allow topic shifts.

209. Audiences like humor.

210. Build up to key points.

211. Don't start a conversation in an accusatory tone.

212. Facilitate and illuminate. Don't enforce rules.

213. Good leadership means doing less and being more.

214. Be conscious of how close you stand to people.

215. Sign up to give a public talk.

216. People tell gossip to get a reaction. Don't take the bait.

217. Avoid unnecessary points in conversations.

218. Apologies only matter if you don't do it again.

219. See something; say something.

220. Include everyone in a group conversation.

221. Admit nervousness.

222. If money means happiness, then you'll never be happy.

223. Don't intrude on personal space.

224. The more weapons you have, the less secure you feel.

225. Never complain, never explain.

226. Self-indulgent speech reveals a lack of character.

227. Talking is a two-way street. Let traffic run both ways.

228. Living the ordinary life leads people back to their true nature.

229. Go outside and scream as loud as possible. Why not let it out?

230. Don't point a fork or chopstick while eating to make a point.

231. Ask questions during dinner conversation.

232. Graceful not grouchy.

233. Use your voice like a toy and play with it.

234. Get another's attention for conversation by lightly touching their elbow.

235. Gazing into another's eyes can cause uneasiness or romance. Know the difference.

236. Entertain but don't monopolize. Leave them laughing.

237. Ask waiters to pronounce difficult food words.

238. Save 100 days of sorrow by being patient in a moment of anger.

239. Respect a verbal attacker.

240. Repeat a person's name to see if you say it correctly.

241. Set the right tone by saying "I need to talk to you."

242. Don't let the acid of anger boil inside. Let it go.

243. Get over anger or sadness by saying something nice to another.

244. Shed light when verbally attacked. Manage it now by telling the truth and not waiting.

245. Exciting, not exhausting.

246. Talking about yourself is boorish behavior.

247. Focus on talking from the stomach not the throat.

248. Engaging conversation is like a well-played ping-pong match.

249. Children mimic those around them. Let them mimic happiness.

250. Chatty, not blabby.

251. Seek compassion, simplicity, and equality in conversation.

252. In family life, be completely present.

253. Sincere, not slick.

254. Life is too short not to show the world the true you. Be open.

255. Wise leaders let others share in winning.

256. Prepare a transition when changing conversation topics.

257. Don't repeat stories to regular conversation partners.

258. Get to the point.

259. Guard against repeating catchwords like "really" or "how fun."

260. Carve your name on hearts, not marble.

261. Speaking slower helps others understand. Practice patience.

262. People bully to gain concessions. Be aware of it.

263. Bad company corrupts good character. Avoid bad influences.

264. Pick the right time for a heart-to-heart talk.

265. Soothe an angry person by saying "I'm sorry you're angry."

266. Don't mumble.

267. Guerrilla commanders only fight on their terms. Their best weapon is intelligence.

268. Lively, not limp.

269. People tend to mimic those leading conversations. Don't be misled.

270. Talkative, not tedious.

271. Lower the volume if people step back.

272. Exhibit humility, not hubris.

273. Handling anger takes a calm approach. Stay cool.

274. True words aren't necessarily eloquent. Eloquent words aren't necessarily true.

275. Respond intelligently to unintelligent conversation.

276. Saying "I don't know" is far superior to false knowledge.

277. Relax what is tense. Reduce what is overflowing.

278. Don't panic when in foreign situations.

279. Understand the healing power of the spoken word.

280. Better to step back than overstep.

281. Production, not promises.

282. Frequent swearing shows a lack of vocabulary variety and becomes boring rather than edgy.

283. Treat talking like the miracle it is.

284. Think character not convenience. Take the extra step.

285. An apology means accepting a mistake that hurt another person.

286. Asking requires a plan. Plan a request.

287. Honest talk reduces worry.

288. A well-place kind word lives forever.

289. Failure is an opportunity.

290. Multiple discussions may be necessary to resolve problems. Don't rush to a conclusion.

291. Don't let others manipulate with fear.

292. Speak up when asked repeatedly "What?"

293. Don't whisper to one person in group conversations unless it's your attorney.

294. Keep in mind the different "characters" you play in life.

295. Ask for help.

296. Bright, not brash.

297. People fearing confrontations enable others to wield power over them.

298. Anger impedes judgment.

299. Over-excited speakers knock drinks off tables or out of peoples' hands. Stay calm.

300. People appreciate consistency. Stay in your lane.

301. Avoid highly technical jargon in conversation, especially in non-technical settings.

302. Avoid passive aggressiveness. Don't say one thing but do another.

303. Telling the truth creates a sense of power. Be honest.

304. Make no excuses when apologizing.

305. Understand the value of non-action.

306. Develop a nonthreatening but neutral face to use in conversations.

307. Uncontrolled emotional outbursts wreck families, friendships, and jobs. Seek balance.

308. Live simply. Don't look for the benefits of more.

309. All things change, so don't hold on.

310. Do not use profane language in front of strangers or children.

311. Criticizing people's clothes, hair, or looks makes you look bad.

312. The real you shows up when the truth does.

313. Not knowing is true knowledge.

314. Pay attention with an open mind.

315. Let people hate you for the truth rather than for lies.

316. Solutions not "sorry."

317. Keep the heart as open as the sky.

318. Speak with confidence, not arrogance.

319. If you look to others for fulfillment, then you will never be fulfilled.

320. Gossip spreads with your involvement.

321. Don't underestimate an enemy. Thinking he is just evil makes you vulnerable.

322. Strategize on a goal. What are the best words to get what you want?

323. Not trusting others makes you untrustworthy.

324. Blaming others makes you look arrogant or guilty.

325. Practice when preparing to give bad news.

326. Pick the right setting for important talks.

327. Sighs, groans, burps, and moans create bad impressions.

328. Provide enough time to discuss important matters.

329. Bad breath, body odor, stale perfume, and smoke affect conversations. Freshen up.

330. Discuss, don't delay.

331. Prevent trouble before it happens.

332. Fluent, not flippant.

333. Hold threatening conversations in public locations if necessary.

334. Credit is we, blame is me. Give credit to others.

335. Calmly determine the next move after a difficult discussion.

336. Offer colorful adjectives, not colorless commentary.

337. Persuasive, not persistent.

338. Admit mistakes and acknowledge hurt feelings when apologizing.

339. Be cautious about giving advice to people you don't know well.

340. Avoid judging others in public.

341. Strive for consistency of character when talking.

342. Silence is better than fillers such as "ahs," "ums," and "hmmms."

343. Don't let eyes wander around the room when talking to someone.

344. Superior attitudes create enemies.

345. Make acknowledgments, not accusations.

346. Avoid personal, religious, or political views in casual conversation.

347. Don't make excuses; if you screw up then own it.

348. Lies are worse than excuses.

349. Reduce me, my, and I in conversation.

350. Must you value what others value?

351. Avoid contentious subjects when drinking alcohol.

352. Mastering others is strength; mastering yourself is true power.

353. Avoid multitasking when talking.

354. Ask new acquaintances if you can call them by their first name.

355. Remain as calm at the end as in the beginning.

356. People who point out your faults are your most benevolent teachers.

357. Greet everyone individually (if possible) when entering a room.

358. Care about people's approval and you'll be their prisoner.

359. Ask permission before bringing a guest.

360. Look at the person speaking to you.

361. Gossiping threatens teller and receiver.

362. Fear is the greatest illusion.

363. Never expecting results means you'll never be disappointed.

364. Trying to make people happy lays the groundwork for misery.

365. Success in life comes with preparation.

366. Humility is common but rugged as a stone.

"Tis a banging of the door behind you—a step forward and you are out of the old life and into the new."

APPENDIX

TALKING IMPROVEMENT PLAN (TIP) & PERSONAL TALKING BRAND (PTB)

Talking Improvement Plan (TIP)

THE TALKING IMPROVEMENT PLAN (TIP) identifies areas of strength and weakness in your English-speaking abilities and provides suggestions to improve.

The program has no time requirements. The amount of effort put in by you determines the amount of progress made. Achieving excellence takes consistent effort so strive for the yinyang balance of persistence and patience.

Maintain an open, mindful attitude regarding your skills. World-class athletes understand the importance of brushing up on fundamental skills. Look to improve both strengths as well as weaknesses. Polishing skills and techniques never hurts.

Best of luck!

Section 1: Assess your skills

Answer the following questions about how you talk.

1. How fast do you talk?
   a.   Extremely fast…a mile a minute
   b.   I speed up when excited
   c.   At an even pace
   d.   Not fast at all
   e.   I am quiet so speed isn't an issue

2. How loud do you talk?
   a.   Very loud…I never need a microphone
   b.   I get loud just not always
   c.   I am not quiet but I rarely raise my voice
   d.   I am quiet as a mouse

3. Do you use facial expressions?

a.   All the time…people know my feelings by my face

b.   I use facial expressions regularly

c.   Once in a while I raise an eyebrow

d.   Never…they call me stone face

4. Do you use your hands when talking?

a.   All the time…I'm like an orchestra conductor

b.   Quite a bit…especially when excited

c.   On occasion to make a point

d.   My hands are either in my pockets or folded across my chest

5. Do you make frequent eye contact when talking?

a.   Always. You can tell a lot from the eyes

b.   Quite a bit. I don't stare but I check people a lot

c.   It depends. Some people I do and others I avoid

d.   Never. I usually look up, down, or to the side

6. Do you touch other people when talking?

a.   All the time. I put my hand on their back or hold their hand

b.   From time to time when the situation feels right

c.   Not very often and only with friends or family

d.   Never. Why would I?

7. Do you stand close to people when talking?

a.   Yes. I feel comfortable being close to others

b.   When I know the person well

c.   Only if the room is loud or I only want one person to hear

d.   Never. I believe in keeping my distance

8. Do you interrupt people who are talking?

a.   Yes, more than I should. Sometimes I just can't help myself

b.   From time to time…especially in excited conversations

c.   Not too much. I let people finish

d.   Never. I rarely say much, so I don't interrupt

9. Are you a good listener?

a.   Not really. I usually carry the conversation

b.   For the most part but my mind does wander

c.   I am a good listener

d.   Since I don't say much, I appear so but often I am thinking

10. Are you comfortable talking to several people at one time?

a.   I can entertain a whole room

b.   Yes I enjoy it but not always

c.   Once in a while but only with friends or family

d.   Not at all

11. Do you like to tell stories to other people that last several minutes while keeping their attention?

a.   I am a great storyteller

b.   Yes, I can do it

c.   On occasion, but I need to feel real comfortable

d.   I could never do that

12. Do you enjoy speaking English?

a.   Very much

b.   Yes

c.   So-so

d.   No, I don't

13. Can you easily change topics when talking?

   a.   Not a problem

   b.   Sometimes I struggle with getting the conversation on point

   c.   Not very good at all

   d.   I say little so the conversation always goes where the other people want it

14. Do stressful or argumentative conversations bother you?

   a.   Not a problem. I have no problem telling a person what I need

   b.   Most times, I can do it. A few people give me problems

   c.   If I get really angry then I can. But most times I just take it

   d.   No. I hate all confrontation

15. Do you struggle finding the right word to accurately express your thoughts?

   a.   No. I have an excellent grasp of English

   b.   Occasionally it takes me a few seconds to express my thoughts

   c.   Yes the combination of a poor vocabulary and nerves stops me

   d.   I struggle all the time

Step 2: Identify strengths and weaknesses

Go over your answers in Step 1 and identify areas of weakness when speaking English. Use the chart below to do a self-assessment of how you talk.

1. Speed

   a.   Too fast

   b.   Too slow

   c.   Too choppy

   d.   No work needed

Other problems/thoughts/ideas _____

2. Volume

a. Too loud

b. Too soft

c. Too squeaky

d. No work needed

Other problems/thoughts/ideas _____

3. Facial expressions

a. Too many

b. Too few

c. Too inappropriate

d. No work needed

Other problems/thoughts/ideas _____

4. Hand gestures

a. Too much movement

b. Too little movement

c. Too jerky

d. Appropriate

Other problems/thoughts/ideas _____

5. Eye contact

a. Too much

b. Too little

c. Inappropriate eye contact

d. Appropriate

Other problems/thoughts/ideas _____

6. Touch
   a.   Too much
   b.   Very standoffish/cold
   c.   Inappropriate touching
   d.   Appropriate
Other problems/thoughts/ideas _____

7. Distance
   a.   Too close
   b.   Too far
   c.   Appropriate
Other problems/thoughts/ideas _____

8. Interruptions
   a.   Too many
   b.   Inappropriate interruptions
   c.   I rarely interrupt others
Other problems/thoughts/ideas _____

9. Listening
   a.   I never listen
   b.   I listen occasionally but miss things
   c.   I am very uneven when it comes to listening
   d.   No problems
Other problems/thoughts/ideas _____

10. Crowds
   a.   I talk too much
   b.   I can do it but don't like it
   c.   I'm silent in crowds
   d.   No problems
Other problems/thoughts/ideas _____

11. Telling stories
    a.   I love telling stories to a group of people
    b.   I'm OK but struggle with timing and keeping people's attention
    c.   I'm really bad at it
    d.   I never try
Other problems/thoughts/ideas _____

12. Transitions
    a.   I change topics too much
    b.   I find it hard to change topics
    c.   I avoid changing topics
    d.   No problems
Other problems/thoughts/ideas _____

13. Pronunciation
    a.   I struggle pronouncing words
    b.   I get excited and my words get twisted
    c.   I mumble, slur, or stutter
    d.   My accent is difficult to understand
    e.   No problems
Other problems/thoughts/ideas _____

14. Bad Character (multiple choices allowed)
    a.   I'm arrogant
    b.   I'm aloof
    c.   I'm selfish
    d.   I'm dismissive of others
    e.   I'm impatient
    f.   I'm mean
    g.   I'm argumentative
    h.   No problems
Other problems/thoughts/ideas _____

15. Confrontations

    a. I'm strong willed and try hard to get my way

    b. Some people make me quiet

    c. When I'm angry I cause problems

    d. I get upset but say little

    e. Never, I hate confrontations

Other problems/thoughts/ideas_____

16. Vocabulary

    a. I have an excellent vocabulary

    b. I could improve

    c. My vocabulary is poor/limited

    d. I struggle with English

Other problems/thoughts/ideas_____

Consider talking to a close friend and going over your results. Do they agree or do they see areas where improvement may be needed?

Section 3: Suggestions for improvement

Area of focus	Rank 1-good/5-poor	Issue	Suggestion
Touch	1-2-3-4-5	Touch or not?	Don't if unsure/cultures vary
		Excessive	Too much is wrong/don't do it
		Situations dictate	Offering hand to help, etc.
		Family/friends	Some expect physical contact
Distance between	1-2-3-4-5	What's right?	Cultures vary/adjust
		Too close	Can cause discomfort/back off
		Too far away	Says "not interested" to others
Interruptions	1-2-3-4-5	Be mindful	Realize when interrupting
		Apologize	Say "sorry" when interrupting
		Too much	Many interruptions is rude
Proper listening	1-2-3-4-5	Mindful	Practice active listening
		Questions	Focus on asking questions
		Other person	Avoid talking about yourself
		Too quiet	No feedback says "I don't care"
Pronunciation	1-2-3-4-5	Practice	Practice mispronounced words
		Avoid	Don't say difficult words
		Names	Ask people to repeat name
		Ask	If unsure ask for help

Appendix

Areas of focus	Rank 1-good/5-poor	Issue	Suggestion
Transition	1-2-3-4-5	Prepare	Think how to change topic
		Use change phrase	Say "that reminds me" etc.
		Wait	Use break to change topic
		Tone	Set right tone with hard topic
Speeches/talks	1-2-3-4-5	Practice	Start with small groups
		Focus	Focus on individuals not crowd
		Outline	Outline, don't memorize
		Physical	Stand tall and breath
		Good hands	Use positive gestures
		Bad hands	Avoid touching face/hair
Telling story/joke	1-2-3-4-5	Practice	Use mirror to practice
		More practice	Tell to 1 or 2 people
		Wait	Tell when time is right
		Timing	Don't rush/set up slowly
		Enthusiasm	Tell with excitement
		Attention	Get audience to listen
		Tone	Change voice/tone for affect
Character	1-2-3-4-5	Study	Study character when talking
		Authentic	Be yourself, open and honest
Confrontations	1-2-3-4-5	Relax	Maintain composure/poise
		Prepare	Know key points/stick to them
		Step back	Listen as much as possible
		Best tool	Intelligence is your best weapon
Vocabulary	1-2-3-4-5	Research	Know words in your profession
		Don't force	Use new vocabulary naturally
		Minimize	Sprinkle difficult words

Section 4: Make a plan

TIP encourages focus on strengths and weaknesses while speaking English.

Examine Sections One and Two and determine a strong point and a weak point in your speaking style. Then look at Section Three for ideas on how to improve.

1. **Strength**: _____
   a. Strategy to improve: _____
   b. Strategy to improve: _____
   c. Starting date: _____
2. **Weakness**: _____
   a. Strategy to improve: _____
   b. Strategy to improve: _____
   c. Starting date: _____

1. **Strength**: _____
   a. Strategy to improve: _____
   b. Strategy to improve: _____
   c. Starting date: _____
2. **Weakness**: _____
   a. Strategy to improve: _____
   b. Strategy to improve: _____
   c. Starting date: _____

Step 5: Track your progress

After working on a strong and weak point for two weeks determine if sufficient progress has been made to move onto other areas.

Answer the following questions to determine progress. If sufficient progress has been achieved then start working on another topic area. If not then further work is required. As with any effort to change, your honest appraisal is necessary.

1. I've been working on the following speaking strength:

_____

2. After my work in this area I feel:
  a. More confident
  b. Less confident
  c. About the same

3. I've tried using the changes in a public setting:
  a. Yes
  b. No

4. Improving this area has been:
  a. Harder than expected
  b. Easier than expected
  c. As expected

5. I can honestly say I have:
  a. Greatly improved
  b. Moderately improved
  c. Stayed the same
  d. Gotten worse

6. I believe the best plan of action is to:
  a. Move on to another area
  b. Continue working on this area
  c. Move on but be mindful of this area when talking

7. Write a short paragraph describing your effort so far in this area including what you've done, ways you've improved, public efforts, and areas that need work.

_____

_____

_____

_____

_____

8. Give yourself a grade (100% to 0%) on the following on your work in this area over the past work period.

    a. Effort: _____%

    b. Improvement: _____%

    c. Public use: _____%

    d. Overall grade: _____%

1. I've been working on the following speaking strength:

_____

2. After my work in this area I feel:

    a. More confident

    b. Less confident

    c. About the same

3. I've tried using the changes in a public setting:

    a. Yes

    b. No

4. Improving this area has been:

    a. Harder than expected

    b. Easier than expected

    c. As expected

5. I can honestly say I have:
  a. Greatly improved
  b. Moderately improved
  c. Stayed the same
  d. Gotten worse

6. I believe the best plan of action is to:
  a. Move on to another area
  b. Continue working on this area
  c. Move on but be mindful of this area when talking

7. Write a short paragraph describing your effort so far in this area including what you've done, ways you've improved, public efforts, and areas that need work.

_____

_____

_____

_____

_____

8. Give yourself a grade (100% to 0%) on the following on your work in this area over the past work period.
  a. Effort: _____%
  b. Improvement: _____%
  c. Public use: _____%
  a. Overall grade _____%

Personal Talking Brand (PTB)

This section assists in creating your personal talking brand by combining talking skills, improvements and goals into a package that strives for excellence. Answer the questions as honestly as possible.

1. What kind of talker are you?

Planner	Manipulator	Leader	Debater
Change agent	Problem Solver	Fighter	Free Spirit
Disinterested	Protector	Boss	Helper
Recluse	Excitement seeker	Entrepreneur	Entertainer
Teacher	Rambler	Thoughtful	Logical

Name 3 including any not listed that fit you:

1. _____ 2. _____ 3. _____

2. What's your best talking skill?

Clear and Concise	Posture	Telling Stories	Humor
Public Speaking	One-on-one	Listening Voice	Sincerity
Focus	Pronunciation	Eye contact	Passion
Politeness	Body Language	Discussing mul-	Friendliness
Facial Expressions	Concern	tiple topics	

Name no more than 2 skills (including any not listed)

1. _____ 2. _____

3. Name one personal goal you want to achieve this year that will improve your personal life not work or school.

Examples: I want to make five more friends this year.

I want to be less nervous when I speak in public.

I want to find a person to marry within two years..

I want to _____

4. Name one professional goal you want to achieve this year involving work, school or professional advancement.

Examples: I want to get a promotion at work this year.

I want to finish my college degree within the year.

I want to improve my ability to give public presentations.

I want to _____

5. Name no more than two positive emotional appeals you have when talking. Include any not listed that fit.

Honesty	Patience	Humorous	Sincerity
Friendliness	Thoughtful	Peaceful	Kindness
Enthusiasm	Intensity	Fun	Intelligence
Care	Maternal	Calm	Helpful
Allure		Financial	Leadership

1. _____   2. _____

6. Why do people enjoy talking to you? What is your talking specialty? Name one including any not listed here.

Examples: **I listen well.**   **I have good ideas.**   **I'm friendly.**
                 I'm smart.   **I'm pretty.**   **I don't argue.**
                  I'm fun.   **I care about others.**   **I enjoy life.**

1. _____

7. To achieve my personal and professional goals the following two areas of my talking needs work. Add any not listed.

Clear speaking	**Posture**	**Telling stories**
Public speaking	**Less shy**	**Listening more**
Focus/attention	**Pronunciation**	**Voice**
Politeness	**Body language**	**Eye contact**
Facial expressions	**Friendliness**	**Being concise**
Discussing multiple topics	**Improve accent**	**Cultural understanding**

1. _____   2. _____

8. My Personal Talking Brand

Now write your Personal Talking Brand using the answers from the previous questions. Here is an example.

> My Personal Talking Brand fits my free-spirit, entertaining personality. I am good at facial expressions and telling stories in a

conversation. The next year I want to make five more friends and finish my college degree in communications. My brand will focus on my ability in public presentations and pronunciation to improve professionalism and build personal relationships.

I believe my friendliness and enthusiasm are assets and I will use them to help me to achieve my goals. I will work on improving voice tone and focus to increase my chances for success.

9. My Personal Talking Brand

Use this to describe your Personal Talking Brand. The numbers in parenthesis (1) denote which answer to use from the questions above. Write the description to fit you. Make it as long as necessary and put in the details you want to fit your brand. Refer to it on a regular basis and update it as you evolve.

My Personal Talking Brand fits my (1) _____ personality. I am good at (2)_____ in a conversation. In the next year I want to (3)_____ and (4)_____. My brand will focus on my ability to (5)_____ and_____ to help achieve my goals.

I believe my (5) _____ and (6) _____ are assets and I will use them to help me to achieve my goals. I will work on (7) _____ and _____ to increase my chances of success.

Conclusion

The world sits at a perilous crossroad in its search for balance.

- Countries produce and stockpile a never-ending supply of weapons but no one feels safe, only nervous.
- Technological advancements steamroll forward but no one feels smarter, only manipulated.
- Wealth grows in the hands of fewer people but no one feels richer, only greedier.
- Politicians spew out righteous and indignant rhetoric to supporters but no one feels right, only intolerant.

The drumbeat of bigger, stronger, faster, richer makes us forget that life's best moments involve sharing conversations with people, whether family, friends, neighbors, strangers or coworkers. A kind, loving, or thoughtful word still brings us more joy than any inanimate object including money.

You and I will leave this world. How do you want to go out? Clutching a gun, fistful of money or smartphone to your sinking chest or in the embrace of loved ones? That love only comes from a life filled with thoughtful words and actions.

Answer this question:

What or who holds the greatest potential for positive change throughout the world?

a. Improved technology
b. More weapons
c. A richer world
d. Political leaders
e. Spoken English

My answer is spoken English. Spoken words between people spread co-operation while technology, weapons, money and politicians spread distrust.

Five years of living in China showed me the enormous potential of a world-wide common language which allows people to share cultures instead of fearing them.

The world's two billion English speakers hold tremendous capacity for unleashing positive global change if they decide to spread love, understanding and collaboration instead of suspicion.

My small effort encourages sharing English words, culture and love in a world sorely in need of positive communication. Do your part by taking the time to talk to another English speaker. It doesn't have to be perfect only open-minded and honest. You'll be amazed by how much so little can do.

I leave you with the words of John Donne.

No Man Is an Island

No man is an island
Entire of itself,
Every man is a piece of the continent,
A part of the main.
If a clod be washed away by the sea,
Europe is the less.
As well as if a promontory were.
As well as if a manor of thy friend's
Or of thine own were:
Any man's death diminishes me,
Because I am involved in mankind,
And therefore never send to know for whom the bell tolls;
It tolls for thee.

John Donne

ABOUT THE AUTHOR
John McGory

International award-winning teacher John McGory works with professionals and students from around the world on improving English-speaking abilities.

The oral English specialist taught at Jianghan University in Wuhan, China starting in 2014, with the 25,000-student school naming him International Teacher of the Year in 2015 and 2018.

The *Seeking Balance* author's experience includes English consulting with Wuhan companies such as CITIC Bank and Johnson & Johnson-China and serving as language editor for the Hubei Province's largest English newspaper, *Changjiang Weekly*.

McGory honed his English-speaking skills as spokesperson and speech writer for the Ohio Supreme Court and as a lobbyist for a large business association before starting his educational consulting career.

He holds a Master's degree in journalism from Ohio University's prestigious Scripps College of Communication and a Bachelor of Science degree in education from The Ohio State University. He has guest lectured at six American and Chinese universities and numerous companies.

The author serves as CEO of the American Speech Company, which produces business, education and government seminars and consults with companies and individuals on creating bigger opportunities through better spoken English.

Go to www.americanspeechcompany.com for helpful English-speaking articles, tips and ideas, company information, or to contact the author.

Please feel free to write a review on Amazon.com regarding *Seeking Balance*. We encourage all comments and appreciate your interest.

www.ingramcontent.com/pod-product-compliance
Lightning Source LLC
Chambersburg PA
CBHW071315090426
42738CB00012B/2706